The Myth of the Great Satan

A New Look at America's Relations with Iran

HERBERT AND JANE DWIGHT WORKING GROUP
ON ISLAMISM AND THE INTERNATIONAL ORDER

Many of the writings associated with this
Working Group will be published by the Hoover Institution.
Materials published to date, or in production, are listed below.

ESSAYS

Saudi Arabia and the New Strategic Landscape
Joshua Teitelbaum

Islamism and the Future of the Christians of the Middle East
Habib C. Malik

Syria through Jihadist Eyes: A Perfect Enemy
Nibras Kazimi

The Ideological Struggle for Pakistan
Ziad Haider

BOOKS

Freedom or Terror: Europe Faces Jihad
Russell A. Berman

Torn Country: Turkey between Secularism and Islamism
Zeyno Baran

The Myth of the Great Satan:
A New Look at America's Relations with Iran
Abbas Milani

Islamic Extremism and the War of Ideas:
Lessons from Indonesia
John Hughes

Crosswinds: The Way of Saudi Arabia
Fouad Ajami

HERBERT & JANE DWIGHT WORKING GROUP ON ISLAMISM AND THE INTERNATIONAL ORDER

The Myth of the Great Satan

A New Look at America's Relations with Iran

Abbas Milani

HOOVER INSTITUTION PRESS
Stanford University   Stanford, California

Hoover Institution Press Publication No. 589
Hoover Institution at Leland Stanford Junior University,
Stanford, California, 94305-6010
Copyright © 2010 by the Board of Trustees of the
    Leland Stanford Junior University
All rights reserved. No part of this publication may be
reproduced, stored in a retrieval system, or transmitted
in any form or by any means, electronic, mechanical,
photocopying, recording, or otherwise, without written
permission of the publisher and copyright holders.

First printing 2010
16   15   14   13   12   11   10   9   8   7   6   5   4   3   2   1
Manufactured in the United States of America
The paper used in this publication meets the minimum
Requirements of the American National Standard for
Information Sciences—Permanence of Paper for Printed
Library Materials, ANSI/NISO Z39.48-1992.⊗

Library of Congress Cataloging-in-Publication Data
Milani, Abbas.
The myth of the great Satan : a new look at America's relations with Iran /
Abbas Milani.
        p.   cm. — (Hoover Institution Press publication series ; 589)
    At head of title: Herbert and Jane Dwight Working Group on Islamism
and the International Order.
    Includes bibliographical references and index.
    ISBN 978-0-8179-1134-8 (cloth : alk. paper)
    ISBN 978-0-8179-1136-2 (e-book)
    1. United States—Foreign relations—Iran.   2. Iran—Foreign relations—
United States.   I.   Herbert and Jane Dwight Working Group on Islamism
and the International Order.   II. Title.
JZ1480.A57I715 2010
327.73055—dc22   2010022846

The Hoover Institution gratefully acknowledges
the following individuals and foundations
for their significant support of the
HERBERT AND JANE DWIGHT WORKING GROUP
ON ISLAMISM AND THE INTERNATIONAL ORDER

Herbert and Jane Dwight
Stephen Bechtel Foundation
Lynde and Harry Bradley Foundation
Mr. and Mrs. Clayton W. Frye Jr.
Lakeside Foundation

For Jean joon

Contents

Foreword

For decades, the themes of the Hoover Institution have re-
volved around the broad concerns of political and economic
and individual freedom. The cold war that engaged and challenged our nation during the twentieth century guided a good
deal of Hoover's work, including its archival accumulation
and research studies. The steady output of work on the communist world offers durable testimonies to that time, and
struggle. But there is no repose from history's exertions, and
no sooner had communism left the stage of history than a
huge challenge arose in the broad lands of the Islamic world.
A brief respite, and a meandering road, led from the fall of
the Berlin Wall on 11/9 in 1989 to 9/11. Hoover's newly
launched project, the Herbert and Jane Dwight Working
Group on Islamism and the International Order, is our con-
tribution to a deeper understanding of the struggle in the
Islamic world between order and its nemesis, between Muslims keen to protect the rule of reason and the gains of modernity, and those determined to deny the Islamic world its
place in the modern international order of states. The United
States is deeply engaged, and dangerously exposed, in the Islamic world, and we see our working group as part and parcel
of the ongoing confrontation with the radical Islamists who

have declared war on the states in their midst, on American power and interests, and on the very order of the international state system.

The Islamists are doubtless a minority in the world of Islam. But they are a determined breed. Their world is the Islamic emirate, led by self-styled "emirs and mujahedeen in the path of God" and legitimized by the pursuit of the caliphate that collapsed with the end of the Ottoman Empire in 1924. These masters of terror and their foot soldiers have made it increasingly difficult to integrate the world of Islam into modernity. In the best of worlds, the entry of Muslims into modern culture and economics would have presented difficulties of no small consequence: the strictures on women, the legacy of humiliation and self-pity, the outdated educational systems, and an explosive demography that is forever at war with social and economic gains. But the borders these warriors of the faith have erected between Islam and "the other" are particularly forbidding. The lands of Islam were the lands of a crossroads civilization, trading routes and mixed populations. The Islamists have waged war, and a brutally effective one it has to be conceded, against that civilizational inheritance. The leap into the modern world economy as attained by China and India in recent years will be virtually impossible in a culture that feeds off belligerent self-pity, and endlessly calls for wars of faith.

The war of ideas with radical Islamism is inescapably central to this Hoover endeavor. The strategic context of this clash, the landscape of that Greater Middle East, is the other pillar. We face three layers of danger in the heartland of the Islamic world: states that have succumbed to the sway of terrorists in which state authority no longer exists (Afghanistan, Somalia, and Yemen), dictatorial regimes that suppress their people at home and pursue deadly weapons of mass destruction and adventurism abroad (Iraq under Saddam Hussein, the Iranian theocracy), and "enabler" regimes, such as the ones in Egypt and Saudi Arabia, which export their own problems with radical Islamism to other parts of the Islamic world and beyond. In this context, the task of reversing Islamist radicalism and of reforming and strengthening the state across the entire Muslim world—the Middle East, Africa, as well as South, Southeast, and Central Asia—is the greatest strategic challenge of the twenty-first century. The essential starting point is detailed knowledge of our enemy.

Thus, the working group will draw on the intellectual resources of Hoover and Stanford and on an array of scholars and practitioners from elsewhere in the United States from the Middle East and the broader world of Islam. The scholarship on contemporary Islam can now be read with discernment. A good deal of it, produced in the immediate aftermath of 9/11, was not particularly deep and did not stand the test of time and events. We, however, are in the favorable position of a "second generation" assessment of that Islamic material. Our scholars and experts can report, in a detailed, authoritative way, on Islam within the Arabian Peninsula, on trends within Egyptian Islam, on the struggle between the Kemalist secular tradition in Turkey and the new Islamists, particularly the fight for the loyalty of European Islam between these who accept the canon, and the discipline, of modernism and those who don't.

Arabs and Muslims need not be believers in American exceptionalism, but our hope is to engage them in this contest of ideas. We will not necessarily aim at producing primary scholarship, but such scholarship may materialize in that our participants are researchers who know their subjects intimately. We see our critical output as essays accessible to a broader audience, primers about matters that require explication, op-eds, writings that will become part of the public debate, and short, engaging books that can illuminate the choices and the struggles in modern Islam.

We see this endeavor as a faithful reflection of the values that animate a decent, moderate society. We know the travails of modern Islam, and this working group will be unsparing in depicting them. But we also know that the battle for modern Islam is not yet lost, that there are brave men and women fighting to retrieve their faith from the extremists. Some of our participants will themselves be intellectuals and public figures who have stood up to the pressure. The working group will be unapologetic about America's role in the Muslim world. A power that laid to waste religious tyranny in Afghanistan and despotism in Iraq, that came to the rescue of the Muslims in the Balkans when they appeared all but doomed, has given much to those burdened populations. We haven't always understood Islam and Muslims—hence this inquiry. But it is a given of the working group that the pursuit of modernity and human welfare, and of the rule of law and reason, in Islamic lands is the common ground between America and contemporary Islam.

E. G. Browne, a scholar of Persian letters and culture, once described Iran as a "hotbed of philosophical systems." This country has taken the currents of the world onto itself yet remains *sui generis* among nations. It has adopted Islam but made it its own, Persianized it, given it its bent for philosophy and art and its sense of history as a play between light and shadow. For nearly two centuries now, Iranians have been engaged in a struggle for and over modernity; they have fought for constitutionalism, women's rights, checks on political power, and a balance between faith and personal freedom. Although they have met setbacks along the way, they have nonetheless persevered.

Stanford professor Abbas Milani brings to the Iranian struggle both immense learning and the authenticity of his own personal background. Born in Iran in 1948, he was formed by the philosophical and political currents that blew through the country in the post–World War II years. Like others of his generation, he felt the pull of the American presence in Iran, but after his education in the United States, he returned to Iran for his academic career—or so he thought. He returned in the 1970s, when the old order, the reign of the Pahlavis, was coming apart. He did time in the Shah's prisons in the company of the Shah's politico-religious opponents who would soon demolish that order and build their own radical utopia. Before long, he would run afoul of the new rulers and make his way to the United States.

In this book, Abbas Milani chronicles the rise of the Islamic Republic, the cruelty of its rulers, the systematic way in which they hacked away their modernist inheritance, and the deliberate manner with which they turned the United States into a demon, a veritable Satan, and an alibi for the regime's failures. He provides a seminal reading of the June 12, 2009, fraudulent elections, which displayed to the world the Iranian people's determination to break out of the grip of political and religious tyranny. Iran's heart and mind, Professor Milani argues, are with modernism; the theocrats in the saddle may win a battle or two, but the yearning for progress that has helped shape modern Iranian history is destined to prevail. He leaves with us a supreme irony: a portrait of a ferociously anti-American clerical regime and a thoroughly pro-American Iranian population, perhaps the most innately pro-American people in the Islamic world.

Fouad Ajami
Senior Fellow, Hoover Institution
Cochairman, Herbert and Jane Dwight Working Group
on Islamism and the International Order

Acknowledgments

This manuscript, as with all I have written before, benefits from the wisdom of many but reflects only my own errors. Sections of the book have earlier appeared in other essays or articles, and in each case I benefited from the astute observations of friends or editors who read and commented on earlier drafts.

I am especially indebted to the professionalism of Barbara Egbert, who copyedited the manuscript, as well as to the staff of the Hoover Institution Press who shepherded the manuscript through the many stages of editing, proofreading, and production. I am also appreciative of Hoover's public affairs department in coordinating media outreach connected with the publication of this book.

I am greatly indebted to three of my students at Stanford—Farbod Farjai, Amir Ravandust and Chuck Stern—for their remarkable tenacity and rigor in tracking down facts, quotes, or sources. For eight years, I have been teaching a course at Stanford on the history of U.S.–Iranian relations, and the comments and questions of students in these classes have helped shaped the arguments of this narrative.

John Raisian, director of the Hoover Institution, had the vision to support the continued examination of not just Iran but of radical trends in the Islamic world; this short book is one fruit of that vision. I am also thankful to Fouad Ajami, one of the directors of the project to study radical trends in the Islamic world, for writing his kind introduction to the book.

In the last few years, I have written several articles with my two colleagues, Hoover fellows Mike McFaul and Larry Diamond. Many of the arguments in this manuscript are no more than a distillation of our on-going discussions and debates.

Finally, it is hard to put into words what I and the manuscript owe to my wife Jean Nyland's erudition, her way with words, and the selfless generosity of her soul. To the other indispensable pillar of my life, my son Hamid, my debt is truly more than words can say.

Abbas Milani
February 20, 2010

CHAPTER ONE

The Iranian Purgatory
The Many Paradoxes of U.S. Relations with Iran

> . . . so shall you hear
> Of carnal, bloody, and unnatural acts
> Of accidental judgments, casual slaughters;
> Of deaths put on by cunning and forced cause
> And in the upshot, purposes mistook
> Fall'n on the inventors' heads . . . .
> **Hamlet**

Two countries, "both alike in dignity," have been at odds for thirty years, fighting several proxy wars, sometimes even engaging in direct military confrontations. The clerical regime in Iran has always partially defined itself in terms of its opposition to the United States. The founder of the regime, Ayatollah Ruhollah Khomeini, used the *Qor'anic* moniker of the Great Satan to refer to America—as much a show of intimidated awe as of embittered animosity at what he imagined was America's mythic omnipotence. Today, not only the regime but its invariably self-serving narrative of U.S.-Iranian relations is facing challenges more serious than any in the past.

Iran is today in a state of political purgatory. It all began with the June 12, 2009, presidential election. Instead of accepting what was widely believed to be a victory by Mir Hossein Moussavi, the regime clumsily tried to steal what was an already rigged election. In a sense, every election in Iran is rigged. A vetting process now conducted by several agencies of the regime, including the twelve-member Guardian Council, ensures that in every Iranian election, no one unacceptable to Grand Ayatollah Ali Khamenei and his cohorts can get on any ballot anywhere in the country. Nevertheless, on June 12, 2009, the regime felt it had no choice but to steal the surprisingly contested election. Some 80 percent of all eligible voters took part. The regime tried to use the high voter turnout as an indication of its legitimacy, but the irrepressible discontent with the announced results led to the most profound crisis the regime has faced since its creation thirty years earlier.

As a result of this crisis, the *status quo ante* is dead but a more democratic future is yet to be born. The tyrannical triumvirate of Khamenei, President Mahmoud Ahmadinejad, and some leaders of the Islamic Revolutionary Guard Corps— increasingly dependent on the military might of the IRGC and the street presence of the gangs of Basij (gangs-cum-militia who control every neighborhood and institution in Iran)—stole the election by declaring Ahmadinejad the winner. Though every indication is that the leadership had planned the electoral heist many months earlier, it was nevertheless caught by surprise by the popular resolve to challenge the regime and its electoral machinations. Since June 12, the triumvirate has used everything from imprisoning and executing opponents and gathering rented crowds for pro-regime demonstrations to creating a limp imitation of the infamous Moscow show trials of the 1930s to try to convince the still-defiant nation that Ahmadinejad actually won and that further resistance is futile. Adding insult to injury, the regime continues to humiliate the opposition by accusing it of being a dupe of the United States. The campaign to elect a reformist president and the resistance to the electoral heist have both been, in the regime's narrative, a "velvet revolution." All such revolutions are, in the regime's paranoid view of the world, masterminded by the "Great Satan."

Historians like Garton Ash cherished the emergence of Eastern Europe's velvet revolutions as a new moment in the history of political change, a new paradigm of revolution. However, the Islamic regime in Iran is portraying the popular upheaval there as nothing but the "machinations of American arrogance." Velvet revolutions have been characterized by their belief in non-violent, non-utopian and pragmatic populism, and by their rejection of the old paradigm of violent, utopian, class-based revolutions. The Iranian Green Movement has been, in its chief characteristics, a version of such a revolution.

Since the June 12 electoral crisis, the composition of power in the clerical regime has changed. The IRGC leadership has consolidated more and more economic, political, intelligence, and military power in its own hands. In the month of November 2009 alone it offered almost $20 billion in cash to buy two of Iran's biggest industrial conglomerates—the biggest auto-maker and the country's telecommunication corporation (which controls all the e-mails, mobile and landline phones, faxes, and Internet access in the country). Attempts by some members of the Majlis (Iranian parliament) to oppose these sales as abuses of laws requiring "privatization" have come to naught. The IRGC is now a state within a state. It has its own intelligence division and its own customs office. It owns and operates hundreds of companies in virtually every field of the economy—from agriculture and mining to banking and oil and gas pipeline construction.

Since the June presidential election, the IRGC has also begun to purge the Intelligence Ministry, replacing independent analysts with its own reliable members and officers. During the presidency of Mohamed Khatami (1997–2005), an attempt was made to "professionalize" the ministry and purge it of its rogue elements (including those who had masterminded the murder of a dozen of the country's top intellectuals). Today, however, those being purged are reportedly those who have refused to accept the theory that the people's resistance since June 12 was masterminded by the Great Satan and its Western allies.

Yet there are signs that many in the regime no longer believe the status quo to be tenable or desirable. A handful of powerful ayatollahs admonished the IRGC for its expanding role in the economy and politics. Some have conjured up Khomeini's last political will, wherein he forbade the IRGC to enter the realms of politics and the economy. Others are criticizing the ruling triumvirate for selling the country cheaply to the Russians and the Chinese, demanding to know what sets these countries apart from the United States and why Iran can have relations with them and not with the United States.

Today, the public row between Ayatollah Ali Akbar Hashemi Rafsanjani and Khamenei may be the most telling example of such a leadership rift. But as early as fifteen years ago, Saeed Hajjarian, then a deputy minister of intelligence, concluded that changing the nature of politics in the country was the only way for the regime to survive. He is credited with masterminding the Khatami reform movement and with articulating the theory that the opposition must mobilize as large a movement as possible and use it to thwart Khamenei and his cohorts, to chip away at their absolutist power. While such rifts make the transition to democracy more possible, they render the work of U.S. policy makers more complicated. The ghost of Iran's increasingly assertive democrats now haunts every negotiation. Khamenei and his allies have made several attempts to heal these open rifts within the ranks of the regime and, in their own words, "bring back to the fold" leaders of the Green Movement and even Rafsanjani. But their attempts have so far been for naught.

In the brutal attempts to suppress the people's peaceful demonstrations, units of Basij have played a crucial role. Called *Lebas Chaksi* or "civilians," they are invariably the most vicious in beating unarmed men, women, and even children. There were rumors of tensions between units of Basij and the police, who more than once sided with the people. It remains to be seen whether the regime's attempt to bribe the Basij— through billions of dollars worth of no-bid contracts and through members' inclusion in the ranks of the regular units of the IRGC—will work, and whether the regime can continue to rely on members as the shock troops needed to frighten millions of peaceful demonstrators. In function and social status, the Basij today resembles the Communist League in the waning days of the Soviet Union. It no longer attracts true ideologues and believers but primarily pragmatists and opportunists. A large number of Basij members seem to have joined the organization only to enjoy the many benefits that come with membership, from easier access to government handouts and jobs to entrance to college for their children and even lucrative management positions. How many belong to this category of the purely pragmatically pious, or even the social climbers, and how long they will remain loyal to a shaky triumvirate remains to be seen. It will be key to the regime's ultimate ability to withstand further challenges to its authoritarianism.

The triumvirate that masterminded the electoral coup in June had been planning for months for the possibility of resistance to its plans. First came a realignment of the IRGC. Instead of having a centralized command, it was broken into thirty-one units: one for each province, two for Tehran. Units of Basij, hitherto autonomous, were placed under the direct command of IRGC units. It was announced that, henceforth, defending against the "domestic threat" and the "soft power" of America and the West would be the main responsibility of the IRGC. After June 12, fighting the "color revolution"— or, more accurately, the democratic will of the people—became the main responsibility of the IRGC and its auxiliaries in the Basij. Basij units became the de facto infantry of the IRGC.

These changes have even affected the IRGC's command structure. Many commanders have been moved and reassigned in the last twelve months. The political dynamics of these changes are not altogether clear. Are they intended to further consolidate Khamenei's hold over the IRGC or are they the result of the IRGC's increased power and independence? Were the many new appointments simply the consequence of factional jockeying in the ranks of the IRGC? The new top commander of the IRGC is an officer named Muhammad-Ali Jaffari. Until recently, he was head of the IRGC's strategic think tank. His expertise, it is said, is fighting "color revolutions." It is said that he is responsible for the IRGC study, commissioned by Khamenei, that mapped out the early stages of all "color revolutions." This study was an attempt to nip in the bud any such movements before they could grow to uncontrollable proportions. Some have suggested that for more than a decade now, Khamenei has had something of an obsession vis-à-vis the fate of East European despots and the intellectuals who often led the movements that toppled them. Khamenei considers himself something of an intellectual and a poet, and not only meets regularly with a group of "court poets," but tries to keep abreast of the writings of the intelligentsia who managed the velvet revolutions elsewhere in the world. As so often happens with despots, it was Khamenei's zeal in obviating any possibility of a velvet revolution that helped beget one, in the form of the Green Movement that took shape in opposition to the electoral coup.

Throughout the post-election crisis, President Barack Obama's administration tempered its comments in support of the movement or in criticism of the regime's brutality. This was apparently in hopes of commencing negotiations with the regime on its nuclear program, as well as a desperate effort to avoid giving the regime any excuse to criticize the United States for meddling in Iranian affairs or to label the democratic movement as a tool of America. For thirty years now, the regime has cleverly used a self-serving narrative of U.S.-Iranian relations to hold America emotionally hostage and put it on the defensive. It has constantly conjured up moments of its controversial and contested history. The White House statement on the occasion of the thirtieth anniversary of the hostage crisis—when radical Islamist students, supported by Khomeini, took over the American embassy and held fifty-two diplomats, soldiers, and staff members hostage for four hundred forty-four days—exemplified the Obama administration's excessive caution. The White House could have offered support to the people's democratic aspirations. It could have confirmed that during the demonstrations orchestrated by the

regime to commemorate the hostage crisis, the people refused
to shout slogans against the United States and instead shouted
slogans against Russia and China. Obama could have ac-
knowledged the statement of the highest Shiite cleric living
in Iran at the time, Ayatollah Hussein-Ali Montazeri, who
apologized for taking over the American embassy and taking
diplomats as hostages. Instead, the White House simply announced that the world "continues to bear witness to the
powerful calls for justice and . . . courageous pursuit of uni-
versal rights" by the people of Iran.

Khamenei showed no appreciation for this diplomatic restraint but responded by once again accusing the Obama administration of empty bombast, hypocrisy, and arrogance.
Not even a child, he said, would be fooled by the president's
empty words. In a dismissive tone, he referred to a letter
written to him by President Obama and said sardonically that
Americans write one thing in letters and do something else
in deeds. A few days later, he let one of his minions tell the
world that the leader at that time saw no reason for direct
negotiations with the Great Satan. In the meantime, bloggers
and Web sites sympathetic to the democratic movement became uniformly critical of American policy, some going so far
as to speak of a "grand betrayal."

Khamenei's visceral distrust and dislike of the United
States has many roots. Understanding the troubled history of
recent U.S.-Iranian relations without understanding these
roots is impossible. The Islamic regime has partially defined
itself by this anti-Americanism, using it as a propaganda tool
to establish itself as the leader of the insurgent Islamic faith.
As Shiites, Iranian leaders are a minority in the Sunni-dom-
inated world. As Iranians, they are surrounded by Arabs who
have no love for Persians—*Ajam* in Arabic, with a hint of the

pejorative always accompanying the term. The clerical leadership in Iran needed a banner that was both appealing to a large swath of Muslims around the world and bereft of any denominational or ethnic baggage. Fighting America has been as central to Sunni members of the Muslim Brotherhood in Egypt as to the Alavite Shiites of Syria and the Salafi "rejectionists" in Jordan. "Standing up" to America and Israel has been the regime's sole banner in its claimed leadership of the Islamic movement. In the weeks after the June election fiasco, just as the regime was facing its most serious domestic crisis, newspapers close to Khamenei began to more regularly call him *Amir-Al-Moemenin Muslemin*—the Caliph of Muslims around the world.

The regime, since its inception, has also defined itself in opposition to modernity and its accompanying secularism and democracy. Khomeini and Khamenei have more than once claimed that secularism and democracy, nationalism and rationalism—even the social sciences—are all poisoned ingredients of modernity, itself a tool of colonial hegemony. Khamenei recently railed against what he pejoratively called the "rationalistic," "materialistic" social sciences of the West. He asserted that they are all founded on the Cartesian idea of skepticism—both anathema to Islamic values and a source for the velvet revolutionary fervor in Iranian youth. Interestingly, his words followed closely those of Hajjarian in his recent post-election show trial. Still unable to speak clearly as a consequence of a failed assassination attempt, Hajjarian had a fellow prisoner read a statement wherein he declared—in a brilliant tone of irony—that he was not guilty but that real guilt lay with German sociologists Max Weber and Juergen Habermas, and that it was Western sociology that was responsible for his fall from orthodoxy. These sciences, he said, inculcate the habit of critical thinking and skepticism and thus undermine faith in *Velayat-e Fagih,* or rule of the highest cleric. (It is a measure of this regime's support for terrorism that the man found guilty of attempting to kill Hajjarian was freed after serving only a portion of his term and in January 2010 was publicly appointed to a prominent government position.) Though there are now more than two and a half million students studying social sciences in Iran, Khamenei ordered a new "cultural revolution" wherein the social sciences should be "Islamicized."

America as "The First New Nation," in the words of American sociologist Seymour Martin Lipset, and as the quintessence of modernity, cannot but prove a nemesis to the likes of Khamenei. He has, like Khomeini before him, more than once claimed that secularism begets heresy and is incompatible with piety. But America is easily the world's most pious industrialized nation; it is a country where separation of church and state is combined with profound piety. French historian Alexis de Tocqueville recognized this combination as the "genius" of American politics. Thus America remains a potent example revealing the lie at the heart of the clerical regime's claim that faithlessness is the inevitable price of secularism and democracy. This is a lie, incidentally, that is shared by every Islamist group around the world fighting for a new Islamist state based on *sharia* religious law.

There is another reason for Khamenei's genuine anti-American animosity. In recent years the United States, as the country that has most steadfastly stood up to the clerical regime, has found a great following among the people of Iran. Much empirical and anecdotal evidence demonstrates that Iran is the only Muslim country where the people, in spite of the ruling regime's rabid anti-Americanism, are favorably disposed toward the United States. For this reason, too, Khamenei cannot but have a visceral dislike of the United States.

The regime's anti-Americanism has yet another root in the structural similarity the regime's ideology shares with the absolutely polarizing worldview promulgated by Soviet Marxism during the cold war. In his seminal work on the origins of Russian communism, Russian philosopher Nicholas Berdiayev used a subtle genealogical method to uncover striking similarities between the tenets of atheistic Leninist ideology and the dogma of Russian Orthodox Christianity. A similar kind of cultural genealogy reveals hitherto overlooked similarities between orthodox Marxist ideology and the tenets of Shiism, as formulated by the Islamic Republic of Iran. In their epistemology or vision of truth, their logic and style of textual exegesis, their organizational commitment to vanguards and hierarchy, their messianic sense of history, their mechanistic aesthetics that places art altogether in the service of dogma, their advocacy of "just war" and "revolutionary" violence, their belief in social engineering and the necessity of creating a "new man," and, finally, in their view of the individual and society as instruments of some higher purpose, Khamenei's Shiism and Soviet Marxism both tap into the same craving for certainty that modernity's celebration of doubt and relativism begets. And they are both equally dismissive of the kind of ambiguities about truth and human nature that have made modern individuals and societies prey to totalitarian ideas and ideologies. As many thinkers and social scientists, writers and poets have reminded us, modernity and its cult of reason beget two forms of society. On the one hand, societies accept the inherent ambiguities in the human condition and affirm the notion that power and laws are the results of a social contract between the ruler and the ruled, and that no one but the people themselves can sign this social contract. The result is a democratic polity where the voice of the people is heard primarily through participation in free and fair elections. On the other hand, there are invariably minorities in modern societies who claim to speak for the people and their general will and "sign" on behalf of the people a "social contract" that places them permanently and unimpeachably at the helm. This begets totalitarian forms of government. Fyodor Dostoyevsky's "Grand Inquisitor" is a brilliant rumination on this existential enigma of modernity.

Totalitarianism's many forms of absolute theology—as noted by German legal scholar Carl Schmitt—are the bastard children of modernity. Soviet Marxism and Khomeini Shiism both claim the monopoly mantle of "true science"—one had Stalin's infamous "dialectical materialism" in mind when it talked of science, and the other has long claimed access to nothing less than the infinite wisdom of God. They both disparage "Western" and "bourgeois" science—Stalin for its lack of materialism and Khomeini and Khamenei for its materialism. In reality, they both disparage science (social and natural) because it begets a rational and inquisitive mind—and such minds, with their "lean and hungry looks," are dangerous to proletarian or pious Caesars.

The air of mythical power incumbent in the moniker Great Satan was a natural result of this worldview. That is why the regime cannot forgo its banner of anti-Americanism, nor can it see itself as anything but in a stage of constant siege in a battle against satanically powerful foes. In the eyes of regime stalwarts, every element of this American "other"—from its individualism and its jeans to its democratic ideals and popular culture—must be resisted. The regime's preparation for what Khamenei believes is its inevitable confrontation with the United States is all-encompassing. It covers everything from supplying arms and training to Hezbollah in Lebanon and the Shiites of Yemen to maintaining a vast network of contacts with Shiite and Sunni groups throughout the Muslim world, united only around the banner of anti-Americanism. The regime's nuclear program is of course the most potent part of its arsenal in its perceived battle with the United States. The focal point of the coming Armageddon for them is obviously between the Great Satan and the government of God on earth.

Today, several thousand units of the Basij are being trained to engage in offensive and defensive actions in what has been called "cyber-jihad." The main focus of the cyber-jihad is the soft power of the United States and other countries of "world arrogance." Classes for the Basij cyber-warriors now include such items as "fundamentals of cyber-jihad and its similarities to Islamic jihad," "semiotics of images and their unconscious impact," "infiltrating cyber-rooms," and the use and manipulations of symbols in political cyber-jihad. In the peaceful demonstrations that followed the electoral coup of June 2009, part of the battle was fought in cyber-space. Iranian democrats used everything from Facebook to faxes to organize demonstrations. The regime countered by setting up its own cyber-war headquarters, calling it, incredibly, *Gerdab*—or the Gutter. It used a machine-generated system of robo-calls intended to intimidate citizens and warn them against participating in future demonstrations. The work of the Gutter is to track down demonstrators and intimidate them by putting their pictures on its Web site. Tehran is now under the watchful eyes of more than twelve hundred cameras. The regime has promised to increase their number, claiming they are for "security and crime prevention." When all else failed, the regime resorted to simply shutting down all mobile and Internet communication in the country. If in June the IRGC had political control of the country's telecommunications system, today it is also its owner.

Unfortunately, not only the Chinese and Russian governments but Western companies—like Nokia Siemens—have been more than willing to sell the regime the software and provide it with the know-how to monitor or shut down "subversive" sites, control and monitor calls and e-mails, and improve its oppressive machinery of surveillance, censorship, and intimidation. Even some American companies have used their subsidiaries in Europe or elsewhere to bypass the American embargo and help the regime with its mischief. Most important of all, by buying Iran's oil and gas, the world continues to empower the machinery of oppression at home and adventurism abroad. Nevertheless, the regime has not succeeded in using this wealth and technology to intimidate the population into docile submission.

As the June 2009 presidential election approached, the regime was faced with a variety of potentially troublesome candidates. It used a variety of tactics to rid itself of this problem and to set the stage for a preordained Ahmadinejad victory. Khamenei reportedly asked two formidable conservative challengers—Bagher Ghalibaff and Ali Larijani—to withdraw from the race. The first was rewarded with an appointment to the politically important job of mayor of Tehran and the second with the job of speaker of the Majlis.

But then Khatami, the two-term reformist president, announced his willingness to run. Polls all showed he would easily beat Ahmadinejad, whose economic failures at home and irrational adventurism abroad had made him highly unpopular. In the months before the election, Ahmadinejad made crude attempts to buy the votes of some of society's most dispossessed. His office gave cashier's checks of about seventy dollars each to anyone who asked. He increased the retirement salaries of some government employees (only to reduce them a month after the election) and, in one case, even gave out sacks of potatoes to buy the votes of members of the lower strata of society. He made numerous trips to the provinces, handing out money he was not constitutionally authorized to give for various projects. Meanwhile, more than a hundred of Iran's top economists complained that he was squandering the windfall that had come to Iran because of the rise in the price of oil. In fact, Ahmadinejad's penchant for squandering the revenue went against the letter of a law that required the government to set excess oil revenue aside in a special account to be used in case of a sudden drop in the price of oil. Ahmadinejad not only failed to deposit this extra revenue, but withdrew from the fund to pay for his harebrained ideas.

Ahmadinejad was following the dictates not of sound economics but of populist despotism. Aside from the many tricks he had learned in this arena when he was the mayor of Tehran, he has also been learning from his newfound friend, Venezuelan President Hugo Chavez. An estimated one thousand officers of the IRGC are stationed in Venezuela, where they try to master the gimmicks used by Chavez to score his electoral victories. Direct flights between Tehran and Caracas, often with only a few passengers, provide a costly sign of the amity between the two countries and a ploy to challenge or embarrass the United States. If Chavez gave away televisions to his potential base among the poor, Ahmadinejad gave them sacks of potatoes. Other trips to Latin America by Ahmadinejad were meant to embarrass the United States, create a coalition of anti-American forces, and occasionally, as in the case of Ecuador, ensure Iran more supplies of uranium.

But crude payouts and anti-American antics notwith-standing, in the weeks before the election Ahmadinejad was losing ground in both the cities and the countryside. Khatami was the problem. To get him out of the race, the triumvirate of Khamenei, Ahmadinejad, and leading cadres of the IRGC orchestrated an elaborate plan of attack. It included every-thing from physically assaulting Khatami after a speech to an editorial in *Keyhan*—the newspaper generally assumed to speak for Khamenei—threatening him with a fate like that of Pakistan's Benazir Bhutto, assassinated at a campaign rally. The threats eventually worked and Khatami, never known for his defiance or bravery, withdrew from the race.

The other early candidate, Mehdi Karubi, was not deemed to be a serious threat. Karubi had been a trusted student of Khomeini. From the first days of the Islamic rev-olution, he held key positions; at times, Khomeini used him for highly sensitive and secret missions. For a while, he was the speaker of the Majlis. Under the Shah, he had spent time in prison as an ally of Khomeini. In power, he remained a constant champion of prisoners' rights and gradually joined the ranks of reformist critiques of the regime. At first glance, Karubi appeared to be an attractive candidate. He had amassed an impressive group of advisors and political activists around him, including some of Iran's best economists—sev-eral of them trained in American universities such as MIT, Harvard, and Stanford, and proposing a comprehensive eco-nomic plan that called for a vibrant new private sector. He offered an impeccably democratic plan and platform. Since losing the last presidential campaign, he had set out to me-thodically create a party and had launched a paper, *Etemad*

Melli,[1] that became the most widely read publication in Iran. However, for reasons impossible to pinpoint, there was no surge of excitement for his candidacy.

The reformists coalesced, not around him, but around the figure of a new candidate, Mir Hossein Moussavi, a dour technocrat who had served as a hard-line Islamic-socialist prime minister during the eight-year war with Iraq. In those days, he had often been at odds with Ali Khamenei, at the time an over-reaching president. For example, when Khamenei was elected for a second term, he worked hard to replace Moussavi as prime minister. Khomeini forbade the change, according to Rafsanjani, leading to much behind-the-scenes tussling between different factions and ultimately an embarrassing defeat for Khamenei. And Khamenei is nothing if not vengeful. He waited almost twenty years and, in the aftermath of the June election, he had his chance to exact revenge on his one-time nemesis.

For almost twenty years, Moussavi had been out of the political limelight. Without much charisma or much of a record, he seemed doomed to fail. Their path, the members of the triumvirate thought, was now paved for victory. They failed to account for three important factors. The first was what Rafsanjani, in a remarkably frank letter to Khamenei before the election, had called "a seething volcano of discontent" in Iran. Second was the ability of the people to unleash the creative energies of the Green Movement and fashion Moussavi into its leader. The third was the resolve of Moussavi, Karubi, and Khatami to resist an electoral coup. Faced with these inconvenient realities, and bent on declaring Ahmadinejad the winner, the triumvirate put all pretense aside, stole the election, and then revealed the brutality that has been the sole reason for its survival.

Events since June 12 have marked at least three crucial developments in Iran, each with important consequences in the complicated arc of its relations with the United States. The fissures within the regime have never been as evident as they are today. The discontent of the clergy with the regime has never been as vocal. Khamenei and Rafsanjani, two of the regime's main architects who had been friends, allies, and partners for fifty years, are now on opposite sides of the political divide. Rafsanjani, commensurate with his well-known caution and opportunism, has still left open the possibility of "returning to the fold" of the regime, thus breaking with those who have given up on this regime. He continues to remain critical of theocracy and its policies, but never beyond a point of no return. Many other top clerics have also publicly criticized regime policies since June 12. Some, like Ayatollah Montazeri, have gone so far as to question Khamenei's moral stature to remain the leader and have declared many official policies to be against elements of *sharia*.

The Obama administration's offer to negotiate unconditionally with the regime has already exacerbated existing policy differences among its ranks. And most important of all, the population, three-fifths of which is under the age of thirty, has lost its sense of powerlessness. Even before the electoral coup, the people were remarkably fearless in articulating their discontent. The election of Obama was received with enthusiasm among this group. "Obama" in Persian consists of three words: Ou, ba, and ma, meaning "he with us." Slogans using this convenient euphony appeared in Tehran and on the Internet Web sites supporting the opposition. Previously, many Iranians considered the regime's tolerance of some public articulation of discontent as a form of what German philosopher Herbert Marcuse called "repressive tolerance," allowing the harmless release of some resentment as insurance against those resentments cohering into a violent revolution. Since June 12, that tolerated fearless resentment has been coupled with a new sense of empowerment. The sight of a couple million like-minded citizens, marching with remarkable discipline, can give even the most intimidated and fragmented citizenry a new sense of power. In Poland, when millions showed up to welcome back their native son, Pope John Paul II, the experience was an invigorating, if not formative, experience for the eventual emergence of the Solidarity movement. For despotic regimes like Iran or Poland of the cold war days, an empowered fearless citizenry is a death knell; they require their intimidated citizens' silence. Ending that intimidation begets an end to such regimes; events after June 12 have gone a long way in ending this intimidation in Iran. Recent attempts by the regime to flex its muscles—from appointing a mullah in every school and ordering arrests, executions, and public show trials, to organizing marches by hundreds of thousands of Basij members and announcing a move to mobilize millions more—are all intended to reestablish that sense of fear and intimidation.

Tehran is a city of between ten and twelve million people. It is estimated that at least one million (according to some reports, close to three million) people came out in the streets for five days to protest what they considered to be a rigged election. There were also demonstrations in many other big cities. (In smaller cities, people were understandably afraid to protest, worried that they would be immediately identified by local units of IRGC and Basij. In big cities, they find safety in numbers.) Khamenei and his accomplices can claim to have won the battle for the election but, as a result of these demonstrations, they have lost the larger struggle for the regime's legitimacy. In despotic societies, so long as the regime continues to have access to the machinery of oppression, it can sustain itself in power and delay the time when new realities translate into a new political structure. While events since June 12 and Khamenei's abdication of his traditional pose of remaining above factional feuds have exacerbated tensions within the regime, and between the regime and the people, it is important to remember that such fissures are endemic to the regime and the result of the paradoxes that define it.

The Islamic Revolution of 1979 was a historic event defined as much by its ironies and paradoxes as by its novelties and cruelties. As a concept, revolution is itself a child of modernity, founded on the ideas that humans have certain inalienable rights and that legitimate power can emanate only from a social contract consecrated by the general will of a sovereign people. As German political philosopher Hannah Arendt argued, before the rise of modernity and the idea of the natural rights of human beings, revolution as a word had no political connotation and simply referred to the movement of celestial bodies. The word took on its new political meaning—a sudden, often violent, structural change in the nature and distribution of power and privilege—when the idea of a citizenry, imbued with natural rights, including the right to decide who rules over them, replaced the medieval idea of "subjects," a passive populace, bereft of rights, deemed needful of the guardianship of an aristocracy or royalty.

In Iran, despite the requisite popular agency of a revolution, events in 1979 paradoxically gave rise to a political order wherein popular sovereignty was denigrated by the regime's founding father, Ayatollah Khomeini, as a colonial construct, created to undermine the Islamic concept of *umma* (spiritual community). Even more ironic is the fact that without President Jimmy Carter's human rights policies, it is hard to imagine the victory of Khomeini and his allies. Nevertheless, after victory, not only did anti-Americanism become an essential part of Khomeini's foreign policy, but he in essence rejected the very idea of the revolution that afforded him power. In Khomeini's treatise on Islamic government, the will of the people is subservient to the dictates of the divine, as articulated by the leader. In this sense, his concept of an Islamic Revolution is an oxymoron and its concomitant idea of Islamic government—*Velayat-e Fagih*—is irreconcilable with the modern democratic ideal of popular sovereignty. On the contrary, *Velayat-e Fagih* posits a population in need of a guardian, much as minors or madmen need guardians. The people are, in other words, "subjects," not citizens. Since the June 12 electoral controversy, which has shaken to the core the foundations of despotism in Iran, regime apologists have gone so far as to reject the very letter of the constitution. They have declared that the leader is not elected by the Council of Experts—the eighty-six-member body of clerics entrusted in the constitution with the job of selecting a new leader and terminating his rule if he proves undeserving—but "discovered." According to this new iteration by Khamenei acolytes, no one—not even the Council of Experts—has the authority to dismiss, or even elect, the leader. Authority is anointed by the Lord, in other words, and can only be taken away by that same Lord. Mere mortals can only "discover" this heavenly design. While the democratic movement has challenged these undemocratic ideas, the regime has tried to give these medieval ideas a progressive veneer by accusing the democratic movement of following slogans and programs proposed by the United States. According to Khamenei and his supporters, the velvet revolution and its ideas, and thus any notions that question the leader's absolute and divine power, are concocted in American think tanks and universities. The indictment against a hundred leaders of the reform movement accused American government, institutions, and universities, as well as Western social scientists and governments, of funding and theoretically formulating the strategy and tactics, the slogans and symbols of the Green Movement.

In the decade before the revolution, Iranian secular intellectuals—some taking their cues and orders from the Soviet Union and its cold war politics, others (like Jalal Al-Ahmad) following the anti-colonial politics of author and psychiatrist Frantz Fanon—paved the way for the clerical regime. They "rehabilitated" clerical opposition to democracy as a steadfast defense of tradition and clerical xenophobia as "anti-colonialism." They offered a revisionist view of Iranian history wherein the clergy emerged as leaders of the all-important, over-emphasized anti-colonial struggle. In this paradigm, fighting "colonialism" is the only measure and most important goal of progressive politics. No wonder then that the regime in recent months has gone out of its way to celebrate Al-Ahmad as the "pivotal" intellectual of twentieth-century Iran. Khomeini and Khamenei have masterfully camouflaged their own "pious" xenophobia as progressive anti-imperialism. Iran's shared border with the Soviet Union and the fact that Iranian Marxists, taking their cues and orders from the Big Brother, cultivated a cult of anti-Americanism and allowed the clergy, particularly Khomeini, to infuse his xenophobia with enough fashionable radical chic terminology to make it appealing to Iranian leftists and to many liberal democrats. And thus America as the First New Nation and the embodiment of modernity, and America as the main culprit in the cold war, morphed into the myth of the Great Satan—a myth whose use and abuse have defined the Islamic Republic of Iran.

The purpose of this monograph is to offer a brief critical alternative reading of the history of America's relations with Iran and to show how little of reality is reflected in the Great Satan myth. Like all enduring myths, this one has some tangible roots in reality. These moments have been used by the regime today, and by Soviet Marxists before, to obfuscate the other elements and construct the myth. It is only by revealing the truth of this history that the lies can be exposed. A new relationship can only begin after the two nations have arrived at a common, critical, and accurate reading of the past. The clerics in Iran have cleverly held many in America and around the world hostage to this self-serving concocted mythology. Debunking the myth and establishing the realities of the complicated history of the two countries' entanglement is the first necessary step in establishing meaningful and equitable relations.

CHAPTER TWO

The Myth of the Great Satan

The Iranian revolution of 1979 moved the political tectonic plates of the region. Its reverberations can still be felt, not just in the region but around the world. The Soviet occupation of Afghanistan can be directly traced to the contours of U.S.-Iranian relations and the victory of the Islamic revolution in Iran. The Soviets calculated that with the fall of the Shah the United States would lose some of its most sensitive monitoring centers keeping tab on Soviet nuclear programs and would try to relocate them to Afghanistan. The Soviet occupation of Afghanistan was in their mind designed to pre-empt America's move into that country. Developments in Iraq, the emergence of Hezbollah in Lebanon, and a new assertiveness of resurgent Islamist groups throughout the world are all directly related to developments in Iran. With the revolution, the United States lost a reliable ally and gained an intractable foe.

The revolution was in no small measure the result of an unusual array of domestic and international forces, from the Shah's strategic misunderstanding of his friends and foes to his failure to fully comprehend the consequences of the socio-economic changes he himself had fostered in the sixties and seventies. Among international factors, U.S. policy had the most profound impact on the rise of the Shah to the height of his power during that time, as well as his fall in 1979. At the same time, his gross mismanagement of the crisis that began in 1977, and the utter disarray in the Carter administration's policy on Iran, allowed that crisis to morph into the revolution that toppled one of America's most reliable allies. In a meeting with the Shah in October 1978, British Ambassador Anthony Parsons offered a surprisingly frank and insightful analysis of why Iran was in turmoil and the regime in crisis. By then the Shah was seriously worried about a possible British or American conspiracy against him. He saw the populist demonstrations as the work of the United States and Great Britain. To remedy the situation, he sought more than anything to satisfy America and Britain. With every passing day, he became more dependent on their advice. He not only met with the two countries' ambassadors several times a week, following their advice on every big and small policy decision, but he asked to meet with them together—lest they conspire against him or each other.

The Shah, Parsons said, had kept the country under "tight discipline for fifteen years while he had pursued his policy of rapid modernization." It was thus inevitable that once this discipline was relaxed, there would be a violent release of popular emotion. The fact that this forced modernization program "had ridden roughshod over the traditional forces in Iran," the fact that it had created "inequalities of wealth and appalling social conditions for the urban poor,"[1] and the fact that even the middle class that had most directly benefited from the Shah's economic reforms was politically disenfranchised and disgruntled with the regime combined to create a crisis and a vacuum of leadership. Forces of tradition, foremost among them the clergy, cleverly used these resentments and rightful demands to realize their dreams of power.

The Shah had altogether ignored the task of both social-izing this new urban class into the ethos of modernity and sharing power with them; the same was true in his handling of the burgeoning middle and technocratic classes. According to a CIA profile of the Shah, he believed democracy "would impede economic development" in Iran.[2] He promised that the time for democracy, albeit in a form he saw fit for Iran, would come in the future. He wagered that he could and should determine the tempo of economic change and the timetable for such a democratic transition; it was, he believed, a "gift" only he could give to the nation. He ignored the advice of economists, politicians, and the American embassy, all of whom warned against too rapid economic development and reminded him of the Iranian economy's inability to prof-itably absorb the new oil windfall.

Much has been made of the "oil curse" and the deforming impact of oil revenues on the fabric of societies overwhelmed by this sudden source of money. Oil has a Janus face: on the one hand, it allows regimes to finance rapid economic devel-opments and create a middle class—thus creating the social requirements for a working democracy—but at the same time it turns the state into an economic Moloch, impervious to popular pressure. The Shah failed to understand the intricate relationship between these two effects of Iran's oil revenues. In fact, buoyed by the sudden infusion of cash, he went on what the Central Intelligence Agency called "a lending binge," giving away hundreds of millions of dollars to anyone who asked, and promised his own people far more than he could deliver. The result was the revolution of 1979.

This "majestic failure,"[3] some believed, was at least partially the result of the chasm that separated the Shah's persona from his actual personality. He was, in the words of Ann Lambton, the eminent British scholar, "a dictator who could not dictate," a weak and vacillating man who pretended to have the authoritarian disposition of his charismatic father. In 1953, when Prime Minister Mohammad Mossadeq challenged him, the Shah first retreated into a debilitating depression and then fled the country altogether. In 1963, when Khomeini first challenged him, it was Assadollah Alam, the prime minister, who stood up to the religious forces and suppressed the movement. He had asked the Shah for a free hand to use the full force of the military to put down Khomeini's zealous supporters. Many observers, including Alam himself, have suggested that even in 1963, without Alam's steely determination and iron hand, the Shah might have caved in.

In 1978, the Shah shrugged off the first signs of massive discontent, claiming dismissively that the cooks in his army could defeat the opposition. According to the CIA, the Shah had a concept of himself "as a leader with a divinely blessed mission to lead his country from years of stagnation . . . supported by a large military establishment."[4] So long as his army of a half-million men (and some women) remained loyal to him, the Shah and the CIA believed, no threat was insurmountable.

For years, it had been something of a mantra in the scholarly and diplomatic analysis of Iran that the Shah's main pillars of power were the military and SAVAK (the acronym for the national security and intelligence organization). Much of the military, particularly the air force and the navy, had been armed and trained by the United States. SAVAK was also created on a model provided by the United States, a model provided to Iran and to other members of what was then called the Baghdad Pact (including Iran, Turkey, Iraq, Pakistan, and Great Britain, with the United States as an observer but not a full member). U.S. advisors, helped by British officers and members of Israel's Mossad intelligence agency, helped train SAVAK. Scholars and diplomats commonly believed that so long as the Shah could rely on the allegiance of the military and SAVAK, he could survive any crisis.

By late 1978, however, the military was in disarray and its leaders either increasingly doubted the Shah's capacity for leadership or, on rare occasions, were seeking to make a deal with the opposition. In early December of that year, in President Carter's nightly intelligence brief, it was reported that an increasing number of generals wanted the Shah to go. By then, the number of deserters in the military was rapidly rising. President Carter's decision in December to send an American general to Iran without telling the Shah[5] sapped any determination the Shah or his generals might have had to fight to keep the monarchy in power. New documents released in 2010 by the British Public Record Office (PRO) show that this general (Robert Huyser) as well as another American general working in the embassy were busy in January 1979 to bring military commanders in contact with Khomeini supporters in Iran. Moreover, throughout the months of the crisis, it was the often-repeated policy of the Carter administration and the British government that the Shah must not use the military against his people but try instead to find a political solution to the crisis.

As an important step in this direction, and as a gesture of appeasement to the opposition, SAVAK was initially purged of its most notorious leaders and agents—and then, in December of 1978, abolished altogether. Even as late as November 1978, many in SAVAK and the army still believed that, given a free hand, they could arrest a few hundred leaders of the opposition, reestablish law and order, and then negotiate with the opposition from a position of strength. In the United States, National Security Advisor Zbigniew Brzezinski shared this view and tried to convince Carter to give the Shah the green light to use the full force of the military. But Carter vacillated until it was too late. The day after Khomeini seized power in Tehran, Carter directed the American embassy there to pursue the possibility of a military coup. "Four-letter words" of anger were the ambassador's only response.

Confused by the contradictory messages he was receiving from Washington, and suffering from the onset of cancer and his own indecisiveness and depression, the Shah rejected the military option. By then it was clear that liberalization and the continuation of Carter's human rights policy would only hasten the end of the Shah's rule. Preoccupied with the Camp David negotiations between Egypt and Israel, Carter entrusted George Ball with the task of assessing the Shah's chances of survival. Ever since the Kennedy administration, when he served as an undersecretary in the State Department, Ball had been a permanent fixture of Washington foreign policy circles, particularly those with Democratic Party links. For a while he was the U.S. Ambassador to the United Nations, but his main area of interest remained the Middle East. His long-held views critical of the Shah had long been known by the cognoscenti in Iran; his often critical views on Israel and on U.S.-Israeli relations were no less known. Now the Shah's chances of receiving continued support from the United States were in his hands. At the same time, it was only after numerous pleas by Egyptian President Anwar Sadat, describing the Shah's despondent mood, that Carter finally found the time to call the Shah and offer him some words of support. It was far too little, far too late.

The George Ball Report, prepared in December 1978, concluded that the Shah's days were numbered. Before long, Carter would invite heads of the British, German, and French governments to the island of Guadalupe to announce his surprising conclusion that the Shah must go. Ball suggested that the United States should dissuade the Shah from any attempt to reestablish his authoritarian position, but convince him instead that his sole chance of survival was to give up all his political and military power and retain only a titular role. Ball also recommended that the United States should urgently "open disavowable (sic) channels of communication with [Khomeini] and his entourage." Long before this prescription, the American embassy in Tehran had established contacts with members of the opposition, particularly allies of Khomeini in Iran.

In spite of the role his own policies had played in the creation of the crisis, the Shah felt betrayed not just by the United States (and the West) but also by the people of Iran. Like a jilted lover, he felt abandoned by the people he thought should love him; like a traditional Oriental potentate, he felt that society owed him a debt of gratitude for the freedoms and the progress he had "given" them.

In reality, during the last fifteen years of the Shah's rule, unprecedented cultural and religious tolerance and freedom existed in Iran. Private lives were free from virtually any governmental interference. The only exceptions were the lives of those who in any way actively opposed the regime (in which case their phones were tapped, their mail was opened, and their movements monitored). Jews and members of the Bahai faith enjoyed virtual equality with Muslims. The economy too was prospering at a remarkably rapid pace, with the gross domestic product and household income regularly showing annual double-digit increases. But for most in Iran's opposition, these cultural freedoms were either a form of "decadent libertinism" or an example of Marcuse's "repressive tolerance." They were seen, in any event, as a mere façade to cover over the more fundamental lack of political democracy.

As for the economy, the opposition either denied or ignored the reality of the improvements, insisting instead on the facts of inequality and corruption. Or else they attributed the changes to some sinister design by imperialists, particularly the United States. Even the Shah's leadership position in the Organization of the Petroleum Exporting Countries (OPEC) and his role in increasing the price of oil were said to be proof positive that he was a lackey of the United States. In spite of hundreds of documents and scholarly analyses that show a bitter conflict between the Shah and the United States over the price of oil, many in the Iranian opposition suggested then, and the current regime continues to claim now, that it was all a charade. The United States wanted to increase the price of oil to squeeze Europe and Japan, the conspiracy aficionados claimed, and thus ordered the Shah to push for higher oil prices! For the Iranian opposition, ultimately, economic progress or cultural freedoms meant little. An omnipotent Great Satan pulled all the strings. On the eve of the revolution, the goal for much of the opposition was political freedom and independence from America.

Moreover, most Iranians touched by modernity—and its notions of the natural rights of citizens—considered the freedoms the Shah had "given" the people to be their inalienable rights. For a hundred years, modern ideas emanating from the French Revolution and its declaration of the rights of citizens had been circulating in Iran. Many of these ideas came to Iran through Russia; as Russian-British historian Isaiah Berlin argued, in Russia democratic ideas were invariably transformed into a more messianic, less liberal, version of their original intent. Nevertheless, the Iranians increasingly saw themselves as "citizens" of a modern polity, not the "subjects" of a traditional fiefdom. The Shah's grandiose rhetoric of the "Great Civilization" and of Iran's new place as a leader of the world, as a country that should soon pass Germany and Japan, helped consolidate this concept of citizenship and all the entitlements it entailed. The Shah, however, in spite of his own grandiose rhetoric, continued to see the Iranians as subjects. As he more than once told his confidante Asadollah Alam, the Iranians needed the strong arm of an authoritarian leader. After the revolution, as the Shah desperately sought a refuge, King Hassan of Morocco was for a while his host. While the two played golf—a passion of the host and a reluctant pastime of the Shah—Hassan told him, "Mohammad Reza, your problem is that you loved Iran but not the Iranian people."

Any decision or policy that benefited the people, the Shah believed, was his gift to the people—a gift for which he expected gratitude from his subjects. He had established an authoritarian system that made him the sole decider for nearly every major economic, political, and military decision in the country. More than once, American diplomats or leaders told him of the dangers of too much concentration of power in his own hands. If you make every decision and take credit for every accomplishment, the Shah was told by both American and British diplomats, in times of crisis you, not the government, will be blamed for all the problems, and people will demand a regime change instead of a change of government. But it all fell on deaf ears. Only a powerful king, the

Shah believed, could take Iran out of its vicious cycle of poverty and backwardness.

As a report by the State Department's Bureau of Intelligence and Research made clear, by the mid-sixties "the Shah is not only king, he is de facto prime minister, and is in operational command of the armed forces. He determines or approves all important governmental actions. No appointment to an important position in the bureaucracy is made without his approval. He personally directs the work of the internal security apparatus and controls the conduct of foreign affairs, including diplomatic assignment. No promotion in the armed forces from the rank of lieutenant up can be made without his explicit approval. Economic development proposals—whether to accept foreign credit or where to locate a particular factory—are referred to the Shah for decision. He determines how the universities are administered, who is to be prosecuted for corruption, the selection of parliamentary deputies, the degree to which the opposition will be permitted, and what bills will pass the parliament."[6]

When his darkening mood and his failing grip on power rendered him incapable of making decisions, as they did in late 1978, the entire machinery of the state, including the much-feared and well-oiled machinery of the military, came to a grinding halt. But to the Shah and most of his supporters, the United States and the rest of the West deserved all of the blame for the revolution. The Shah felt that America's decision to allow Iran to fall into the hands of what he called a group of "Marxists, terrorists, lunatics, and criminals" was a betrayal that far exceeded "the giveaway at Yalta"[7] to Soviet dictator Josef Stalin in 1945.

The Shah's indecision and the profound contradictions in U.S. policy stood in sharp contrast to Ayatollah Khomeini's clear and early appreciation of the structural nature of the crisis, the democratic nature of the movement, and America's desire to "bring about a responsible government that not only meets the needs of the Iranian people but the requirements of [America's] own policy." The Shah's paralysis—induced as much by his paranoia as by the medications he was taking while undergoing chemotherapy—was more than matched by Khomeini's resolute and ruthless Machiavellian guile. Around the time Ball concluded that the Shah was not likely to survive, the British government reached the same conclusion, deciding on October 30, 1978, that the British government "should start thinking about reinsuring."[8] When the U.S. and British governments began to "reinsure" and tried to establish ties with leaders of the opposition, the only force they found that could, in their judgment, keep the country from falling into chaos—or into the Soviet orbit—was Khomeini and his coterie of clerics. By then Khomeini had put on a charm offensive, sometimes preaching in the mode of a Sufi mystic, other times wearing the mantle of a democratic leader. His allies among the Iranian intellectuals in the United States, in Iran, and in Paris—where he spent his last months of exile— helped this "democratic sell."

In the months before the revolution, Khomeini exhibited exemplary discipline in maintaining his democratic façade. In contrast, the American embassy in Tehran showed remarkable gullibility when it concluded that Shiite clerics like Khomeini were capable of creating a democratic polity in Iran, and keen to do so. In Paris, Khomeini did not refer to his undemocratic idea of *Velayat-e Fagih*; instead, he repeated more than once that the next government after the Shah would be democratic and that the clergy would have no role in any of its political institutions. There would be freedom for all and coercion of none, he promised more than once. He could certainly find passages in the *Qor'an* to support this liberal proposition. It is common knowledge that *Qor'anic* verses have different dispositions. Those composed while the Prophet was in the city of Mecca, where he had few followers, are tolerant in attitude and poetic in tone. Those composed in Medina, where Mohammad was the head of state, were stern in disposition and tone. In Paris, Khomeini opted more for the verses of Mecca. He quoted the verse in the *Qor'an* that is similar to Thomas Jefferson's views on religious freedom, saying, "There is no coercion in matters of faith." He told the German newspaper *Der Spiegel* that "our future society will be a free society, and all the elements of oppression, cruelty, and force will be destroyed." A few days earlier, on October 25, he promised that women will "be free . . . in the selection of their activities, and their future, and their clothing."

To add further poignancy to this democratic pose, Khomeini allowed a few ambitious Western-trained aides (like Abol-Hassan Bani-Sadr, Sadeq Gotb-Zadeh, and Ebrahim Yazdi[9]) to become the Parisian public face of his movement. At the same time, unbeknownst to much of the world, he had already appointed a few trusted clerics in Tehran—nearly all of whom had been his students in earlier years—to a covert Revolutionary Committee that managed the day-to-day affairs of Khomeini's followers.

Eventually, Khomeini's democratic promises were transformed into the clerical despotism of *Velayat-e Fagih*. There was in the style and substance of his Paris pronouncements an air of Peter Sellers' portrayal in *Being There* of Chauncey Gardiner—simple-minded innocence masquerading as profound, saintly wisdom. The media and most Western intellectuals were seduced by a kind of romantic infatuation with the exotic East, the novelty of a Sufi sage shaking to the very foundation the Peacock Throne and overthrowing an American ally. But beneath Khomeini's appealing, albeit disingenuous, façade there lurked the steely determination of a despot keen on riding a democratic wave to the deeply undemocratic shores of *Velayat-e Fagih*. Chauncey Gardiner turned into a modern-day Savonarola, railing against the corruptions of modernity and democracy. When asked about this blatant transformation, and about the incongruence between the despotic reality of his rule in Iran and the democratic promises of his Paris period, he declared with surprising nonchalance that in Paris he had engaged in the Shiite practice of *Tagiyeh*—dissimulation in the service of the faith and the faithful.

As a result of this carefully calibrated campaign, much of the world, including the U.S. embassy in Iran, was duped enough to conclude that "the Islamic movement dominated by Ayatollah Khomeini is far better organized, enlightened, and able to resist communism than its detractors would lead us to believe."[10] While Khomeini's movement was surely more organized and better able to resist communism, the claim of being "enlightened" turned out to be dangerously fatuous. America's hope of living amicably with a "responsible government" it had helped bring to power turned into a nightmare that still continues thirty years later.

CHAPTER THREE

Purposes Mistook
America and the
Islamic Revolution

The movement that overthrew the Shah and brought Khomeini to power was democratic in nature and aspirations. Some 11 percent of the total thirty-eight million population of the country at some time participated in the movement, compared to 7 percent and 9 percent, respectively, in the French and Russian revolutions.[1] Slogans of the day were unmistakably democratic as well. Between 38 percent and 50 percent of the slogans were directed against the Shah, while between 16 percent and 30 percent favored Khomeini personally. At best, 38 percent asked for an Islamic republic— and none for a clerical regime.[2] The most common slogan called for independence, freedom, and an Islamic republic. Nearly absent from the scene in these days were calls for "Death to America" and the virulent anti-Americanism of the clergy once in power, as well as "Death to Israel" and the recurrent anti-Semitism that has occasionally reared its ugly head among some in the regime. In fact, Khomeini's allies and representatives met regularly with officials of the American embassy, promising the "responsible government" they knew their American interlocutors wanted to hear.

In the months leading to the collapse of the Shah's regime, Khomeini grabbed the mantle of a populist leader. Instead of espousing his true intentions and ideology, he took on the ideological guise befitting the leader of a democratic movement. He "out-Lenined" the Leninists of the communist Tudeh Party and used them to destroy the democratic opposition. As Rafsanjani makes clear in his daily journals, leaders of the party met with him regularly, always with the excuse of "passing intelligence" to the regime about the opposition. But as invariably happens, the killing machine the party had helped oil eventually turned against the party itself. In an attack surprising only in its national and meticulous scope, Tudeh Party leaders and sympathizers were rounded up in every corner of the country. True to its dogma, the party of course blamed the United States and the West for this surprisingly successful roundup, claiming that the CIA and British intelligence had passed on information about the party to the clerics.

Khomeini also outmaneuvered the democrats, who invariably underestimated him—either because they believed Khomeini's zany ideas were ill-fitted to the complexities of Iranian society, or because they were mesmerized by his charisma and the promise of a share of power. Leaders of the National Front, whose presence in the provisional revolutionary government was intended to reassure the United States of Khomeini's democratic intentions, were foremost among those deceived by this promise of power. There was, aside from crass political calculations, a historical reason for this befuddlement.

Iranian democrats, as well as the Marxists, were children of modernity, imbued with the spirit of the Enlightenment. To them, religion was either the "opium of the masses" or, at best, a relic of a bygone era when revelation ruled reason and humanity wallowed in the Dark Ages. Modernity, in both its totalitarian and liberal democratic iterations, had ushered in the Age of Reason and pushed what remained of religion to the private sphere. Science and rationality would, Enlightenment philosophers surmised, eclipse reason and superstition. In Iran itself, during the Constitutional Revolution of 1905, secular democrats and clerics had united to fight despotism, but after victory the clergy were more or less marginalized. The same, many secular democrats hoped, would happen again, and the clerics would be confined to their traditional religious role.

Khomeini and his cohorts proved adept not only at mastering the complex machinery of state but at marginalizing their democratic and radical allies after victory. More than once, Khomeini and his followers declared, with some glee, that 1979 was "payback" for 1905; the first time the clergy were used by the democrats, and now they used them. But as it soon became clear, the clergy had more than just payback in mind. They had elaborate designs for re-establishing the age of revelation and divine legitimacy and dismissing as flawed the rule of reason in human affairs, particularly in the realm of law and jurisprudence. All they had lost as a result of modernization—from control of the judiciary to control of the educational system—they now reclaimed. The battle for democracy in Iran, in other words, has been not just a political struggle over who rules the country but also a battle between reason and the rule of men and women on the one hand and revelation and the rule of God (and his viceroys) on the other. If in 1905 this battle was revolutionary for its time, there is something absurdly anachronistic about Iran fighting it again in 1979—in an age social scientists call the third wave of democratization and in the era of the digital information revolution.

In 1905, when these paradigms faced off for the first time, most of the top Shiite clerics sided with advocates of constitutional monarchy, arguing that until the return of the Twelfth Imam (now in "occultation," or hiding), there can be no "Islamic government." In this long period of occultation and waiting, constitutional democracy, they said, is the best form of government for Shiites. Only a minority of clerics at the time took a position similar to the one later suggested by Khomeini, i.e., that the goal of Shiites must at all times be to establish an "Islamic government" wherein *sharia* rules.

During that Constitutional Revolution, the United States had only a marginal presence in Iran. Its entanglement with the cause of the revolution was more personal than political. In the words of one of the leaders of the revolution, a "young American, in the person of young Baskerville, gave this sacrifice for the young constitution of Iran."[3] Howard Baskerville was a Nebraska-born American missionary-turned-educator who fought and died on the side of Constitutionalists on April 19, 1909, at Tabriz. Thousands of the city's besieged citizens lined up in the streets to watch the funeral. Baskerville had worked at the American Memorial School run by missionaries in Tabriz—by then the virtual capital for forces advocating a constitutional government. Several of the leaders of the movement had earlier been students in the American school. Though the American consul general tried publicly to dissuade Baskerville from participating in the revolution, the young Christian missionary not only insisted on participating but agreed to lead a particularly dangerous charge against enemy lines.

In those days, and for decades to come, Iran's democratic movement saw the United States as a distant but reliable ally. It was in fact Iran's reformist prime minister Amir Kabir who in 1850 first established diplomatic ties between Iran and America. His hope and plan had been to use the new distant ally as a counterbalancing force against Iran's two colonial nemeses: the Russians and the British. This favorable disposition toward America continued until early 1953, when the United States was involved in the effort to overthrow the popular government of Mossadeq.

In the months leading to the 1979 revolution, the two Shiite paradigms that had faced off in 1905 were once again fighting for domination, this time pitting Khomeini's radicalism against Ayatollah Kazem Shariatmadari's pragmatism. Born in the province of Azarbaijan, the predominantly Turkish-speaking region of Iran, Shariatmadari has yet to receive his rightful and lofty place in the pantheon of Shiite clergy who tried to modernize the faith and thwart the rise of Khomeini-style radicalism. On the eve of the revolution, Shariatmadari was the highest-ranking cleric living in Iran. While ostensibly united with Khomeini, behind the scenes he warned the Shah and the United States of the grave dangers facing Iran if Khomeini were to come to power. He paid dearly for his vision and valor. Khomeini, notorious for his inability to forgive or forget even a hint of disagreement or disloyalty, breached one of the most inviolable principles of Iranian history: protecting the relative autonomy of the clergy and the sanctity of their homes and seminaries. He not only put Shariatmadari under house arrest, but ordered goons and paramilitary forces to attack his home and ransack his seminary. He also declared Shariatmadari "unfit to remain an ayatollah." He even forced the revered septuagenarian to appear on television and, in a show reminiscent of the cruelest days of Stalin, "apologize" for his "sins." Before long, Shariatmadari died—probably as much of heartbreak as of a heart ailment. He was buried in the dark of night, with no public funeral or memorial permitted. Like Baskerville, he died in the fight for democracy. But unlike in 1905, this time the United States was seen by all sides as a key player, in close contact with Shariatmadari, and working behind the scenes to bring about a more democratic government.

In Paris, Khomeini continued to pay lip service to democratic principles. The fact that the Shah and his SAVAK had banned Khomeini's books for decades made his effort to hide behind this fictitious persona easier. Moreover, Khomeini was nothing if not a disciplined politician. Even his book on the subject of *Velayat-e Fagih* was said to have been compiled by his students from their lecture notes, affording him "plausible deniability."

Velayat-e Fagih claims humans are incapable of sound decisions on their own. Like minors who need the "guardianship" (*Velayat*) of parents, people too need the guardianship of the jurist. It is a theological incarnation of the Platonic idea that the "demos" are incapable of sound political judgment and need the guardianship of a philosopher. If for Plato human reason is the key to this philosophical wisdom, for Khomeini it is revelations in the *Qor'an* and in the *Hadith*— words and deeds attributed to the Prophet and his twelve male progeny, called the Imams—that are the keys to justice in this passing world, as well as salvation in the realm of the infinite.

Velayat-e Fagih is equally undemocratic in the way it purports to achieve and maintain its legitimacy. Khomeini posits that legitimacy for this guardianship is divine in origin and not dependent on the consent of the people. In Iran, he made his theory even more undemocratic by introducing the concept of *maslahat* (expediency) and insisting that his words and *fatwas* on what is expedient at any time trump even the fundamentals (*usul*) of *sharia* and Islam.

About six months after Khomeini's return home, the American embassy in Tehran reported that he and a handful of clerics in Qom were "now making decisions on all matters of importance." They were feeding the fractured feuding of the democratic forces, using a rising militant anti-Americanism to neutralize many in the Iranian left. The most brazen mark of this anti-Americanism came in November of 1979, when students occupied the American embassy. These students assumed a role similar to the Red Guard for Mao Tse-tung in the Cultural Revolution; their own chosen moniker, "Students Following the Line of Imam," was redolent of the Chinese madness from 1966 to 1976. The occupation of the embassy was also used by Khomeini to further weaken and eventually dismiss the democratically inclined provisional government he had earlier appointed. In later months, he and his allies also cleverly capitalized on the chaos and crisis caused by Saddam Hussein's decision to attack Iran to consolidate their hold on power. In November 1979, Khomeini used a pliant Constituent Assembly to pass, not the promised democratic constitution, but a new one founded on his ideas about *Velayat-e Fagih*—a constitution in which he was granted, as Supreme Leader, more despotic powers than the Shah he had just replaced.

As many recent memoirs, reports, and interviews by Iranian political figures of the time have now revealed, it was Khomeini who was most responsible for the prolonged occupation of the American embassy. Moussavi was at the time a rising star in the new regime and became Khomeini's beloved prime minister on October 31, 1981. Now a leader of the Green Movement, Moussavi claims that it was in fact Khomeini "who changed what was initially supposed by the students occupying the embassy to be a three- or four-day event into what he himself called a new 'second revolution'." The occupation of the embassy, along with the eight-year war with Iraq, allowed Khomeini to politically liquidate his more liberal and radical fellow-travelers and completely marginalize the opposition. Throughout these machinations, his increasingly strident anti-Americanism was the one constant element of his ideology. To accomplish this, he simply adopted the cold war rhetoric of Stalinism about imperialism, keeping intact the structure, and merely changing the lexicon. Thus, imperialism became "arrogance" (*estekbar*), the proletariat became the "dispossessed" (*mostazafin*), and "brother" replaced comrade.

There was more than mere expedience at work in this adaptation of Stalinist rhetoric to Islamic ideas. As mentioned in Chapter 1, there are, in fact, a surprisingly large number of similarities between Khomeini's version of Shiism and the Stalinist iteration of Marxism. Both use the individual as a tool of abstract historic forces; both claim a monopoly of truth; both posit that this truth is the purview of a minority (the clergy in one, the party in the other), and both suggest that access to this "truth" legitimizes the minority's claim to absolute rule. Both accept a body of texts as sacred and absolute in their veracity and both accept a citation from the source in lieu of—indeed, as more powerful than—any rational argument. Both afford demonic powers to the "Other" and both believe in a messianic vision of history—the Twelfth Imam in one and the proletariat in the other. For both, the interests of the current generation can be sacrificed by fiat for some distant future "good" and both accept as legitimate— indeed, praise as virtuous—violence in the service of their own ends. For both Khomeini and Stalin, the social contract theory of law and the state are meaningless because, for both, the ruler receives his legitimacy from a source outside—or more accurately, above—society (history for Stalin and God for Khomeini).

Ayatollah Montazeri, once a close ally of Khomeini and the spiritual father of the opposition movement until his death in December 2009, has not only apologized for saddling the nation with a despotic concept of *Velayat-e Fagih* but has repeatedly tried to offer a new reading of the concept, one that he claims was the original intent of the framers of the constitution.

Montazeri repeatedly declared that the only legitimacy of the leader comes from the people. This stands in contrast to the claims of Khamenei and his sycophantic allies, who now claim that the leader is "discovered" and not "elected" by the Council of Experts and that his "acquired divinity" is his sole source of legitimacy and cannot be challenged or ended by mere mortals. In language reminiscent of Jean-Jacques Rousseau's "Social Contract," Montazeri argued that politics is "the business of the people" and that the leader receives his power primarily through a contract with the people. But it was not Montazeri's relatively benign iteration of *Velayat-e Fagih* that was put into practice by Khomeini and his successor Khamenei. Instead, both men have seen the concept as a mandate to interfere in every detail of the state and to rule not only with an iron fist but with a totalitarian claim to an absolute monopoly of divine truth. For both, fighting the Great Satan is the seal of their sacred mission.

Iran's democratic dream was once again delayed. Revolutionary terror tried to deracinate the democratic flowering that blossomed briefly after the revolution. In the months after the Shah's fall, there was no censorship in the country. Hundreds of papers and magazines, each presenting a different perspective, were published. Books banned for the last thirty years suddenly flooded the market. In cities and villages, no less than in governmental or private offices, committees elected by the people took over the daily management of the machinery of power and management. Political parties were free to operate. A "hundred flowers" were abloom (reminiscent of China in 1956), and it was precisely their power and promise that frightened Khomeini. Gradually, and often violently, Khomeini dismantled the democratic machinery, replacing it instead with a complicated and despotic clerical structure. The committees that had been democratically elected by the people were replaced by committees dominated by clerics appointed by Khomeini, invariably housed in mosques. Before long, these new committees were placed in charge of surveillance and suppression. In the country, as in each institution, a dual power structure emerged. There was a provisional revolutionary government, and its appointed ministers advocated normalized relations with the United States. Real power, however, was invariably in the hands of anointed "imam's representatives" (*namayandeye imam*), and for them anti-Americanism was emerging as the pivot of their revolutionary rhetoric. The regime's killing machine began by executing members of the *ancien régime*. When faced with criticism of the kangaroo courts, summary trials, and speedy executions, the Khomeini who a few months earlier had promised the rule of law in a democratic Iran now declared in brazen disregard for both, "All one needs do with criminals is to establish their identity, and once this has been established, they should be killed right away."[4]

The power and authority of these courts and committees were ensured by the growing strength of the newly created Islamic Revolutionary Guard Corps. Instead of dismantling the predominantly royalist army, much of it armed and trained by the United States (which would have created five hundred thousand unemployed, armed, and trained potential foes of the regime), Khomeini kept the military intact and simply retired, exiled, or executed nearly the entire class of generals. Younger, more zealous officers were placed in command positions. At the same time, more and more money and power were placed in the hands of the IRGC. Ironically, in spite of the clerical regime's anti-Americanism, U.S. policy had, at least inadvertently, played a crucial role in preparing the ground for the rise of Khomeini to power. More than any, the three administrations of John F. Kennedy, Richard Nixon, and Jimmy Carter played pivotal roles in pursuing policies that eventually led to the fall of the Shah and the rise of clerical power. In the heat of the hostage crisis, Montazeri, by then the second most powerful cleric in Iran after Khomeini, suggested that the regime should release the American hostages before the November presidential elections in the United States. We owe much of our success, he told Khomeini, to Carter's human rights policy, and releasing the hostages before the election will not only repay the debt but make it less likely that a Republican will become president. Khomeini rejected the idea outright. The hostages remained in custody for four hundred forty-four days and were released minutes after Ronald Reagan took the oath of office. Was it fear of Reagan that caused the strange timing of the release, or was it part of a secret deal between some in the Reagan campaign and the clerics in Iran to delay the release of hostages until after the election? After months of investigation and millions of dollars, a special committee of the U.S. House of Representatives, entrusted with the task of investigating whether there was such a deal—a so-called October surprise—came away unable to conclude unanimously that any such deal was made. And even if there had been, it still remains a mystery why the hostages were not released soon after the election in November 1980 but rather were held until just minutes after Carter left office in January 1981. Could it be that the timing was signature Khomeini politics and a cruel attempt to embarrass and dishearten an already defeated Carter?

Even though Carter had suspended diplomatic ties between Iran and the United States, Iran's geo-strategic importance ensured America's intense interest in political developments in Iran even after the release of the hostages. If up until World War II Britain and Russia were the dominant outside forces in Iran, after 1941 the United States became the clearly dominant outsider.

The Persian malady of conspiracy theories—attributing every major event in the modern history of the country to some pernicious and pervasive foreign force, whether the British, the Freemasons, the Communists, the "Zionist-American" conspiracy, or now the American design for a "velvet revolution"—has only added poignancy and confusion to the debate about America's role in Iran's domestic politics.

Belief in conspiracy theories, or "heated exaggerations, suspiciousness, and conspiratorial fantasy," is founded, as American historian Richard Hofstadter has argued, on a "paranoid style of politics."[5] Such beliefs and theories are themselves an enemy of democracy. They posit and produce a passive citizenry, willing to accept that forces outside society shape and determine the political fate of the community. A responsible citizenry, cognizant of its rights and responsibilities, is a foundational prerequisite for democracy. But conspiracy theories absolve citizens of responsibility for their own action and fate, placing all the blame on the "Other." The anti-colonial rhetoric of the Left, with its tendency to place all the blame on the "Orientalist" West, helped nurture this nativist tendency to forego self-criticism and instead blame the "Other." And after World War II, and particularly after the onset of the cold war, America was invariably this guilty "Other."

Ironically, this conspiracy proclivity played an important role even in fomenting the 1979 revolution. The United States was imagined to be an almost omnipotent outsider that not only controlled the Iranian economy and the military but also played a determining role in shaping the contours of political developments. Khomeini was reported to have religiously listened to the nightly news broadcasts of BBC, Voice of America, and Radio Israel. On the other hand, American embassy officials reported numerous meetings with the Shah, other regime officials, and members of the opposition at which the main subject was America's allegedly formative role in supporting and encouraging the opposition. This theory remained potent, despite the U.S. government's many steps to reassure the Shah and regime officials of its continued support. As Austrian-British philosopher Karl Popper has argued, an indispensable characteristic of all historicist anti-democratic theories is that they are not falsifiable. Any attempt to offer empirical or rational proof against the theory is already "explained" and dismissed by the theory—and conspiracy theories become forms of historicism when they reduce the complicated flux of history to the machinations of one actor or conspirator. In the mind of the Shah and other advocates of conspiracy theories, American attempts to deny their alleged omnipotence were in themselves "proof" of the veracity of the conspiracy theory. Attacks by leaders of the Islamic Republic against "American machinations" in Iran today and their refusal to accept U.S. denials of interference in Iran's domestic affairs are at least partially a continuation of this proclivity.

As American embassy officials knew, the exaggerated power they possessed in people's minds was a two-edged weapon. It gave a misleading impression of America's ability to influence, but it also afforded Americans more of a chance to "offer advice and see them effectively implemented."[6]

And so, by the time of the 1979 revolution, no country was deemed as powerful in Iran as the United States—blamed by the royalists for the revolution and for betraying the Shah, and considered a foe by the new regime, accused of conspiring to bring back the Shah and fomenting a civil war. As a U.S. embassy memorandum written on the eve of the revolution made clear, "the 'secret hand' theory which is deep in the Iranian grain . . . blames the U.S. (among others) for Iran's many problems."[7]

In spite of this clearly exaggerated perception, the policies of different American administrations were crucial in different moments of post–World War II politics in Iran. The controversial George Ball Report stated the obvious when it observed in 1978, "All parties are looking to the United States for signals." If the resolution of the crisis was, according to Ball, now dependent on U.S. policy, he was no less unequivocal about the role of the United States in creating the crisis: "We made the Shah what he has become. We nurtured his love for grandiose geopolitical schemes and supplied him the hardware to indulge his fantasies." Ball went on to say that once the Nixon Doctrine "anointed [the Shah] as protector of our interests in the Persian Gulf," the United States became dependent on him. "Now that his regime is coming apart under the pressures of imported modernization," not only must the United States unambiguously end the Nixon Doctrine but it must pressure the Shah to give up much of his power and "bring about a responsible government that not only meets the needs of the Iranian people but the requirements of our own policy."[8] Surely Nixon and his doctrine played a role in the genesis of the crisis that led to the 1979 revolution. What Ball failed to point out was the no less critical role the administrations of Kennedy and Dwight D. Eisenhower played in creating the dynamics that eventually helped beget the crisis.

Though Iran's relations with America began in the mid-nineteenth century, it was only after the Second World War that the United States began what the eminent scholar James A. Bill has called its entanglement with Iran—one consistently fraught with incident. In 1922, there was an attempt by the Iranian government to invite American oil companies to invest in Iran, but the effort came to naught. The death of an American citizen in 1924 at the hands of an angry mob, apparently insulted by his decision to take a picture of a religious site, created tensions between the two countries. In the late thirties, the mistaken arrest of an Iranian diplomat in Washington temporarily ended diplomatic ties between the two nations. Reza Shah, ever watchful of a slight by Western powers, considered the arrest not just a breach of diplomatic protocol but a grievous affront to him and the Iranian nation.

In these same years, the work of a few other Americans was reinforcing the positive image of America in the minds of Iranian nationalists. There was the work in the twenties of American financial advisor Dr. Arthur Millspaugh, who was given a free hand to clean up the notoriously corrupt and inefficient bureaucracy. His direct, even brash, demeanor allowed his corrupt enemies to undermine his efforts. Sometimes even honest Iranian officials found it hard to tolerate his behavior. There was also archeologist Arthur Pope, who enjoyed the support of Reza Shah and his son, Mohammed Reza Shah. His study of Iranian art led to the preparation and publication of his magnum opus, *Survey of Persian Art.* With the help of other American archeologists and universities, Pope and his wife, Phyllis Ackerman, were involved in uncovering and celebrating parts of Iran's pre-Islamic past. Their work went hand-in-hand with the attempts of the Pahlavi dynasty to create from these shards of memory and history a new national identity for Iranians founded more on the pre-Islamic grandeur of empire than on the influences of the Islamic millennium.

Finally, in these years before World War II, Dr. Samuel Jordan created what became easily Iran's most influential high school for much of the twentieth century. Like Baskerville, he was a graduate of Princeton's Theological Seminary. He lived more than four decades in Iran; like other missionaries before and after him, soon after his arrival in Iran he gave up Christian proselytizing in favor of modern pedagogy or, more specifically, "character building." Some of Iran's first schools for girls, nursing schools, and modern hospitals were built by these missionaries turned pedagogues. None of these institutions can compare with what Jordan and his wife, Mary, created in 1889, initially called the American College of Tehran. They ran this institution for almost forty years, giving it up only when the government of Iran took over all missionary schools in 1939. The Jordans' motto was elegantly simple and poignant: "the young Oriental, educated in Western lands, as a rule gets out of touch with his own country . . . We adopt the best Western methods to the needs of the country, while we retain all that is good in their own civilization."[9] In their attempt to combine the best of Iranian and American cultures, they advocated "the dignity of work . . . the virtue of service . . . democracy, and the equality of women." They published the first bilingual student magazine in Iran, as well as a magazine specially dedicated to women's questions. The school was later renamed Alborz. Although Jordan was forced to give up his stewardship of the storied institution in 1939, a disproportionate part of Iran's elite continued to be trained there. In many other cities, from Shiraz and Isfahan to Tabriz and Hamedan, American missionaries established schools and hospitals, creating an increasingly more positive image of America in Iran.

World War II changed everything in Iran, and its relationship with the United States was no exception. In the mid-thirties, Nazi Germany began a concentrated effort to find a foothold in Iran and the rest of the Muslim world. The Nazis tried to convince Reza Shah that they considered the populations of Iran and Germany to be members of the same master race. Thus, Iran could be a partner in Hitler's designs for a thousand-year Reich. At the same time, the Nazis told the Islamic clergy that Hitler was a devout convert to Islam and was keen on expanding the faith. Some clergy, "encouraged" by German operatives, went so far as to claim that Hitler was the Twelfth Imam, the missing messiah. Posters with pictures of Hitler on one side and Shiite Imams on the other appeared around the country. German spies were also busy creating a network of armed militia they could eventually use if Nazi forces advancing in the USSR reached the Iranian border. The militia would be the fifth column Germany needed to topple the government should it try to resist a Nazi takeover of Iran and its oilfields.

But even more than fifth columns and Reza Shah's pro-German sympathies, the Soviet and British governments were concerned about securing Iran's transnational railroad, argu-ably the most crucial link to supply the Soviets' beleaguered Red Army. It is a measure of U.S. stature in Iran at the time that when, in August 1941, British and Soviet forces finally attacked and all but overnight occupied Iran, Reza Shah sent an urgent plea to President Franklin D. Roosevelt and asked for "efficacious and urgent humanitarian steps to put an end to the aggression." Roosevelt took some time to respond, and when he did, offered little comfort to Reza Shah. The key passage of Roosevelt's response turned out to be the last sen-tence, where he declared that the Soviet Union and Britain had both promised to leave Iran as soon as hostilities ended.

Even before the Soviet-British attack and the urgent plea to Roosevelt, Iran had tried to get the United States interested in Iran by offering to buy eighty American war planes, asking Standard Oil to explore for oil in Iran, and offering American companies generally an opportunity to invest in Iran. It was, of course, all to no avail. But on the eve of the Second World War, the U.S. alliance with Britain and the Soviet Union was strategically far more important than any short-term invest-ment opportunity in Iran.

Before long, the United States had more than three thou-sand soldiers stationed in Iran, all primarily involved in the work of making the railroad run efficiently. By the end of World War II, Iran was called the "Bridge to Victory" in reference to the millions of tons of material and weaponry that went through Iran to the USSR.

From the first days of the war until the arrival of General Patrick Hurley, Roosevelt's special emissary to Tehran, there was ongoing tension between the British ambassador, Sir Reader Bullard, and the U.S. embassy over treatment of the Iranians. Bullard had a tendency to behave like a bully and talk like a colonial master. His dispatches from Tehran reek of haughtiness; the American ambassador and Hurley both found Bullard's discourse and demeanor objectionable. By the time Roosevelt arrived in Tehran for the famous Tehran conference, Hurley had already developed some strong ideas about the contours of future U.S. policy in Iran.

After discussions with Roosevelt, Hurley was entrusted with the task of formulating the president's ideas for a new experiment in democracy promotion in Iran. Known as Hurley's Report, the new policy viewed Iran as "a country rich in natural resources," poised to become an independent nation ruled by a government "based on the consent of the governed." It could become an experiment in helping Muslim nations become more democratic. Noble American blood, Hurley said, must not be shed to prop up the moribund British empire or to help realize the hegemonic designs of ascending Soviet imperialism.

Nothing came of Hurley's Report. The State Department dismissed Hurley's proposals as "baloney" and the death of Roosevelt and onset of the cold war together created a new dynamic in America's relations with Iran. Many scholars have in fact suggested that the dawn of the cold war came to Iran in the form of the Azerbaijan crisis. As the end of World War II neared, Stalin succumbed to the desires of his infamous chief of police, Lavrentiy Beria, who had insisted for some months that the Soviet Union must secure rights to the enormous oil and gas reserves beneath the northern provinces of Iran. In a memorandum dated July 6, 1945, Stalin ordered the "organization of a separatist movement in Southern Azerbaijan and other provinces of Northern Iran."[10] Stalin wanted to use the separatist movement and the continued Soviet occupation of parts of Iran as bargaining chips for the oil rights to Iran's northern region.

Attempting to create a legal obstacle to the Soviet Union's insistence on these rights, Dr. Mossadeq, an influential member of the parliament at the time, sponsored a bill that made it illegal for the Iranian government to negotiate any oil deal while hostilities lasted. The Tudeh Party—created after the fall of Reza Shah by pro-Soviet Marxists in Iran—opposed Mossadeq's bill, unless it included an exclusion clause about what the party ideologues shamelessly called the "Soviet Union's legitimate rights" in Iran.

Iran filed a complaint with the United Nations, becoming the first nation to ask the Security Council to intervene in a crisis. Britain and the Soviet Union, for different reasons, were against Iran pursuing its U.N. complaint. The Soviets knew they would be the losers in the debate and the British worried that discussions about northern oil rights might eventually jeopardize Britain's monopoly rights in the south. The United States, on the other hand, vigorously supported Iran's request that the Security Council take up its complaint against the Soviet Union.

After a while, the United States directly demanded that the Soviet Union evacuate Iran's territory. President Harry S. Truman claimed that he had issued an ultimatum—the first and only one in the era when the United States enjoyed the monopoly of nuclear weaponry in the world. Scholars have suggested that Truman was actually referring to a stern message, not an official ultimatum, delivered by the American embassy in Moscow, making it clear that Soviet occupation of Iranian territory was not an acceptable option. Stalin's army did withdraw from Iran, under a combination of factors: pressure from the United States, opposition by Iranian nationalists, and the promise of a concession by Iran's prime minister at the time, Almad Qavam al-Saltaneh. Iran thus became the only case in the years immediately after the Second World War in which the Soviet Union withdrew from a territory occupied—or "liberated" in the parlance of the time—by its Red Army.

In the Azerbaijan crisis, the United States played an instrumental role in preserving the territorial integrity of Iran. Yet it is an often forgotten moment in the history of U.S.-Iranian relations. Instead it is the U.S. involvement in the overthrow of the Mossadeq government that has left its lingering effect.

Many factors have made it almost impossible to objectively analyze America's role in the overthrow of Mossadeq in 1953. These include the anti-American zeal of the cold war and the influence of Iran's Tudeh Party in shaping intellectual discourse in post-war Iran. Another factor was the CIA's self-adulating account, in which it took credit for what happened in August 1953—followed by its claim to have lost all documents relevant to its role when ordered by Congress to release them! Then there was the remarkably bombastic account of Kermit Roosevelt, the CIA operative in charge of what was called "Operation Ajax" in Tehran—an account, incidentally, that he published only when the Shah's regime was about to fall. Before then, for years, he used the good offices of the Shah to enrich himself as a middleman for American companies doing business in Iran. Still more factors include Mossadeq's near-mythic stature in Iranian history and the refusal of British intelligence to release its documentation on the event. The Shah insisted that what happened on August 19, 1953, was a "national uprising" in his support; Mossadeq's supporters claim that what happened that day was brought about by a small band of prostitutes and pimps, helped by a handful of officers all bribed by the United States. Finally, there is the Islamic Republic's clever abuse of a self-serving tale of the Great Satan overthrowing a popular and democratically elected government. All these factors have combined to make it almost impossible to "historicize" the debate and permit a cool and impartial analysis of the degree of American responsibility for the fall of Mossadeq. But even a cursory look at events and existing documents reveals the many flaws in the tale that is still so popular.

When Mossadeq nationalized Iran's oil in 1951, he considered the United States an ally in what he knew was his own collision course with Great Britain. In fact, it was the Truman administration that blocked British plans for a military takeover of the oil fields and the refinery in the city of Abadan. For two years, the United States made every effort to find a negotiated solution to the crisis between Iran and Britain. Both the Shah and Britain, more than once, came to the conclusion that Mossadeq was in fact working in collusion with the United States. By late October 1952, the Truman administration came to the conclusion that Mossadeq would not compromise and that the United States should accede to British suggestions that the two countries work together to overthrow his government.

If by then the United States was willing to contemplate the idea of a coup, it was because of several changes in Iran and around the world. Stalin was dead and, in the words of an advisor to President Dwight D. Eisenhower, the United States needed to "assume a firm and steady hand everywhere throughout the world."[11] Iran's dire economic situation—the result of its inability to carry and sell oil directly—was further complicated by Mossadeq's diminishing popularity at home. His alliance with the clergy had collapsed by 1953. On the one hand, Mossadeq had rejected the demands of Ayatollah Abol-Gassem Kashani, the leader of the Islamist forces, for more influence on the government—including the right to appoint some ministers and the enforcement of more Islamic laws. Among the clergy's demands were restrictions against members of the Bahai faith. Bahais have been the bane of Shiite clergy for over a hundred years. The origins of the faith go back to the teachings of Mohammed Bab in mid-nineteenth-century Iran. For his claim of offering a new prophetic vision, Bab was put to death on the orders of Shiite clergy. From these early teachings of Bab the Bahai faith emerged in the twentieth century. Some scholars have considered the new faith the much anticipated "reformation" in Iran. Shiite clergy, on the other hand, have refused to ever engage Bahai as a religion, dismissing it instead as a "Zionist/imperialist" cult, created to undermine Islam. To his credit, Mossadeq resisted all of these pressures and stood up to the clergy. On the other hand, many factors combined to weaken Mossadeq and render him politically vulnerable: the dire economic situation, the dubious support of the Tudeh Party with its changed attitude toward Mossadeq (from an "old vulture of American imperialism" to the lion-hearted leader of the anti-imperialist struggle), and the increased radicalism of some of Mossadeq's supporters (foremost amongst them Dr. Hossein Fatemi, the fiery foreign minister and journalist).

One of the events that made Mossadeq constitutionally vulnerable was his decision to dismiss the parliament through a referendum, an act which Iran's constitution rendered of dubious legality. More important, as many of his advisors reminded him, with no parliament in session the Shah would have the right to dismiss the prime minister and make a recess appointment for his replacement. Mossadeq had believed that the Shah would not dare dismiss the popular prime minister. He was wrong.

The United States, relying on the contacts earlier established and nurtured by the British, planned to support the Shah's effort to fire Mossadeq and appoint General Fazlollah Zahedi as his replacement. Mossadeq, forewarned about the Shah's plans, arrested the officer who delivered the letter of dismissal. No sooner had the Shah learned of the arrest than he fled the country in a small plane, landing in Baghdad. Every indication on the eve of August 18, 1953, was that the planned attempt to replace Mossadeq had failed. The Shah left Baghdad for Rome, where he began contemplating life as a gentleman farmer in Connecticut. The U.S. ambassador, Loy Henderson, hoping for plausible deniability, had left Iran for a holiday a few days before the coup attempt.

The United States called it Operation Ajax. For the British, it was apparently more personal. They called it Operation Boot. Kermit Roosevelt was dispatched to Iran with plans for regime change, plans that Eisenhower called the stuff of dime novels. On August 18, after the State Department and the CIA concluded that the attempt to topple Mossadeq had failed, Henderson rushed back to Tehran and was taken directly from the airport to see Mossadeq, who showed a "certain amount of smoldering resentment." His many jibes "hinted that United States was conniving with British in an effort to remove him as Prime Minister." Nevertheless, he went on to have an hour-long discussion with the ambassador. Mossadeq denied having seen any royal decree dismissing him as prime minister—a false claim, as he had in fact seen the decree when he ordered the arrest of the man bearing the message—and went on to claim that "for some time now" his position had been "that the Shah had no right" to call for "a change of government."[12]

But on August 19, suddenly and unexpectedly, the tide turned against Mossadeq. The U.S. embassy reported an "unexpected strong upsurge of popular and military reaction" to Mossadeq. This upsurge, in the embassy's view, was caused at least in part because "people of all classes were disgusted at the bad taste exhibited by anti-Shah elements" and also by their worry about "at least a temporary alliance between Mossadeq and Tudeh." Moreover, the people had "become thoroughly tired of the stresses and strains of the last two years."[13] Followers of Mossadeq of course blamed only the CIA.

Whatever the cause, and whatever the role of the CIA and the American embassy in changing the tide, the Shah was returned to power but stigmatized as a ward of the United States. The United States became more and more involved in the day-to-day affairs of the country. The Eisenhower administration provided millions of dollars of aid to the new government, hoping to allow it to quickly improve the economy and thus assuage remaining popular resentment against the overthrow of a popular government. The fact that the Shah insisted on putting Mossadeq on trial not only increased tensions with the opposition but further tarnished the U.S. image. Mossadeq used the trial to mock the Shah but he also lambasted the U.S. and British governments for interfering in the domestic affairs of Iran.

In politics, image is reality. After August 1953, the United States was seen as the Shah's patron, held responsible for every decision he made. The most sensitive issue was of course the oil negotiations. Ultimately, a consortium of oil companies, whose shares were more or less equally divided between the United States and Britain, signed a long-term contract with the Iranian government. A year after those fateful August days, Vice President Nixon traveled to Tehran. Despite being met with student demonstrations, he began a life-long close friendship with the Shah at this point.

As early as 1958, the CIA and the State Department were convinced that unless something drastic was done in the realm of politics and the economy, Iran was heading toward a revolution. In September 1958, the National Security Council met to discuss a new "Special National Intelligence Estimate" which claimed that the Shah's regime was "not likely to last long." It was decided that the United States must work hard to "convince the Shah that the most immediate threat to his regime lay in internal instability rather than external aggression."[14] He must, in other words, reduce his "preoccupation with military matters" and focus more on social development.

The intelligence estimate asserted that the main opposition to the Shah was "the growing educated middle class," discontented with "Iran's antiquated feudal structure and the privileges of the ruling classes."[15] They were further angered by the corruption of the military, political, and civil service authorities. Nepotism and charges of corruption against members of the royal family and the Shah himself were also causes of dismay. Such charges were so rampant at the time that the U.S. embassy organized a joint committee with members of the British embassy to look into the allegations and estimate the size of the Shah's fortune. The picture they drew was not complimentary to the royal family. The report said that the Shah, as well as his family, had numerous investments in nearly every sector of the economy. All of this led the United States to propose a series of far-reaching changes in Iran. The Shah was to be pressed for prompt, "meaningful political, social, and economic reforms."

It was further decided that should the Shah resist these proposed changes, the United States would take immediate steps toward "developing appropriate contacts with emerging non-communist groups."[16] The United States was convinced that unless there was a controlled revolution, creating more democracy and a market economy, a radical revolution—one that might benefit the Soviet Union—would be inevitable. Despite many developments over the next eight years, the Shah's precarious position remained remarkably the same. In 1966, the State Department's Bureau of Intelligence and Research "pointed to basic difficulties for the Shah . . . The realities of the future will not include the indefinite polarization of one-man rule; in some fashion that cannot yet be discerned, it appears likely that the Shah will confront a choice between allowing greater participation in government or seriously risking a fall from power."[17] This 1966 prognosis showed remarkable prescience, particularly when contrasted with the CIA's analysis in 1978, concluding that Iran was not even in a pre-revolutionary stage. This failure to foresee the Islamic revolution of 1979 must be considered among the more serious intelligence failures of the twentieth century. It can be at least partially accounted for by the 1965 decision of the U.S. government to succumb to the Shah's pressure and cease all contacts with members of the opposition in Iran. An auxiliary of this policy was a drastic reduction in the number of intelligence officers working in Iran. It is estimated that by the early seventies their number had returned to pre-war figures.

The 1958 analysis led to a series of U.S. proposals to the Shah. They were planned by a diverse group of scholars and statesmen from such places as Harvard, the Rockefeller Foundation, and the World Bank, as well as agencies within the U.S. government. They altered the economic and political face of Iran and the foundation of the Shah's basis of support. A market economy replaced the semi-feudalism of the post-war years. It was hoped that the authoritarianism of the period would also give way to a more democratic polity, with the Shah assuming more and more the role of symbolic figurehead stipulated in the constitution.

One measure of America's anxieties in 1958 about the future of Iran and of its desire to convince the Shah of the urgency of the situation was the U.S. embassy's decision to keep silent when it was informed by an Iranian general that he intended to organize a coup against the Shah's authoritarianism. The coup leader was Valiollah Qarani, at the time the head of military intelligence. His accomplices were a group of more than thirty other officers, government officials, and journalists. They planned to seize power, force the Shah to play a merely symbolic role, and appoint as prime minister the Shah's old nemesis, Ali Amini. The coup attempt failed— most probably because British intelligence informed the Shah. Nonetheless, not only was Qarani given a surprisingly light sentence but, within two years, as a direct result of U.S. pressure, Ali Amini was indeed appointed prime minister, with a mandate to bring about reforms and a rapprochement with the Shah's opponents. It is important to note that, in addition to members of the secular opposition, Qarani was in close contact with the Shiite clerical leadership. Grand Ayatollah

Kazem Boroujerdi, at the time the unquestionable leader of the clergy, was working behind the scenes to reduce Qarani's sentence.

When the State Department talked of middle class and moderate opposition to the Shah, it meant primarily the National Front created by Mossadeq in 1949 and suppressed after the events of August 1953. Ironically, although the United States had been involved in the overthrow of the Mossadeq government, starting in the late fifties it began to see Mossadeq's followers as the necessary agents for a more democratic Iran. Starting in 1959, the United States put the Shah under increasing pressure to reconcile with this group. In 1978, on the eve of the revolution, those pressures were renewed and reached fever pitch. Unfortunately, the National Front leaders failed to capitalize on these opportunities both in the early sixties and on the eve of the revolution. It was Khomeini more than anyone else who used this American proclivity to his own benefit. The fact that his appointed prime minister and nearly every one of the ministers of the 1979 provisional revolutionary government were from the ranks of the Freedom Movement—the religious element of the National Front—testifies to Khomeini's ability to sense what the United States wanted, his knack for tactical compromise, and, finally, his confidence that he could wrest power from the liberals when he was ready.

If a coalition between the Shah and the National Front failed, it was not all the fault of the National Front. The Shah too was adamantly against the idea of reconciliation. Even in 1978, faced with the end of his dynasty, he was less than enthusiastic about forming such a coalition. In June 1978, in a private meeting with Western diplomats to describe his decision to liberalize, he engaged in "vitriolic denunciations of

the old National Front" and made it clear that it was beyond
"the lines of political acceptability."[18] Still later, when he had
no choice but to beg from a highly weakened position for a
coalition with those same leaders, he refused to accede to the
key demands of the only two National Front leaders who
would agree to cooperate with him. The first was Gholam
Hossein Sadiqi, arguably the last serious chance for the survival of the monarchy. The Shah said no to Sadiqi's request
to stay in Iran but out of politics. Shapour Bakhtiyar was the
next leader willing to forgo past animosities and enter a coalition government to save the country from what he called
the "coming dictatorship of [clerical] sandals." The Shah undermined Bakhtiyar's chance of survival when he declined the
request of General Fereydoon Jam, a key member of the proposed cabinet, to turn over the operational command of the
armed forces. The Shah in fact "stubbornly insisted not only
on retaining his role . . . of commander-in-chief . . . but also
on controlling the military budget."[19] Thus, the only officer
who could have potentially held the military together and
under the command of a Bakhtiyar government left Iran in
disgust. It took the military thirty-six days before it turned
against Bakhtiyar and tried to make its peace with the mullahs, who seemed poised to take over the reins of power. It
was in 1962 that the Shah told the American ambassador that
a National Front government "would be a precursor of communist takeover," as that organization has been "badly infil-
trated by communists."[20] When American officials raised the
issue of the National Front's membership in a new coalition
government, the Shah stated, "flatly . . . he could not live
with a National Front Government whose first act would be
to abolish SAVAK."[21] The leaders of the National Front, the
Shah went on to say, have "no purpose except to come to

power." In 1978 the Bakhtiyar government did abolish SA-VAK, but this gesture was no longer enough to appease the movement.

Aside from the hackneyed argument that the National Front would pave the way for communism, the Shah also informed American officials on numerous occasions that in Iran the king had "always been the center of power." He genuinely believed that the monarchy was "the only form of government that can bring Iran into the modern world" and that if this transition were to be realized, he must rule with an iron fist, preferring "economic progress and social reform" over "the flowering of democratic political institutions."[22] In 1961, cognizant of the Kennedy administration's keen interest in introducing reforms in Iran, the Shah told the American ambassador that if there were to be any meaningful reform in Iran, it had to come under the aegis of the Shah and no one else. He also made it clear on numerous occasions that "he would abdicate rather than accept [the] position of a fig-urehead."[23] That was why in 1961 the Shah found appointing Amini, rather than sharing power with the National Front, the lesser of two evils; the Kennedy administration did believe that Amini's appointment was the only step available in the direction of more stability and democracy in Iran. Even after the revolution, while he was in exile, the Shah held on to his belief that the National Front leaders were either dupes or tools of communism. In his *Answer to History* he repeated his mantra about the role of communists in running not only the Front but the clergy as well.

The effort to force a democratic marriage of convenience between the Shah and the opposition began in earnest with Amini. Supported by the Kennedy White House, Amini did in fact create the semblance of a coalition government. Lapsed communists and inactive members of the National Front joined a few other members of the secular opposition to form a new cabinet. Amini insisted on having more power and independence than previous prime ministers, and in this he had the full support of the U.S. embassy in Tehran. Iran's dire economic situation—the government's desperate need of a loan of $35 million—afforded the Kennedy White House a powerful bargaining position. Even then, Amini still did not have complete freedom to form his cabinet. The most controversial member of his cabinet was easily Hassan Arsanjani. Like Amini, Arsanjani was an old hand in Iranian politics but, unlike Amini, he had been unabashed in his criticism of the Shah. He was a charismatic orator, a muckraking journalist, a self-styled socialist by avocation, and a lawyer by vocation. In the Amini cabinet he was in charge of land reform and the ministry of agriculture. If Qarani had succeeded in his coup attempt, Arsanjani was slated to lead the same ministry.

The Arsanjani appointment became far more important when it became clear that implementing land reform would be the centerpiece of Amini's plans for the "controlled revolution" he had come to lead. Among the reforms suggested by the United States, land reform had a pivotal role. The Amini plans also fit more or less perfectly with what the Shah himself had been suggesting for some time. A few years earlier, the Shah had tried to have legislation passed allowing the government to undertake such reforms but the clergy, led at the time by Ayatollah Boroujerdi, objected strenuously, and the bill was tabled. The death of Boroujerdi and the appointment of Amini together created the right moment to commence the much-discussed land reform, a reform primarily intended to end absentee landlordism.

There is something of a consensus among scholars and politicians, landlords and peasants that Arsanjani's radicalism and charisma, his ambitions and his political acumen made existing plans for land reform far more radical than initially intended.[24] When American embassy officials showed concern about Arsanjani's increasing radicalism, Amini reassured them by suggesting that such rhetoric was initially needed for "taking the wind out of the sails of the National Front."[25] At an appropriate time, Amini assured the American ambassador, "he would accept [Arsanjani's] offer to resign."[26]

While many in the regime supported Amini's changes—eventually called the White Revolution or the "Shah and People Revolution"—there was considerable opposition to it. The opposition came from the landed gentry who were losing their properties, from the clergy who objected to any policy that questioned the sanctity of private property or allowed women the right to vote and enter the political domain, and finally from the military, who believed Amini would cut the military budget and pave the way for Soviet influence. At least two generals—Hadjali Kia and Teymour Bakhtiyar—contacted the White House and sought America's support for a coup in favor of the Shah and against Amini. President Kennedy personally instructed the U.S. government to use all means necessary to discourage these two generals "from initiating any action against the Amini government."[27]

On the other hand, many of Iran's moderates and supporters of democracy dismissed the Amini-Shah changes as cosmetic. Radical forces believed the Shah neither willing nor able to make any serious reforms. Yet another figure questioned the wisdom of the land reform from the perspective of long-term economic and political development. He was known as a planning and economic prodigy, and thus his democratic vision has been eclipsed by the substance and stern style of his management of banks and economic plans. His name was Abolhassan Ebtehaj. Ever since his appointment as director of the Plan Organization in 1955, he had survived in power simply because of the Shah's continued support. By 1961 Ebtehaj's luck had run out and he ended up in prison.

Even in prison, Ebtehaj never shied away from expressing his often unique, sometimes contrarian views. When he learned about the Shah's plans for land reform and his upcoming trip to the United States, he decided to write a pithy "personal and confidential" letter from prison to his "friends in America," hoping to convince them to stop the Iranian government's plans for land reform. Ebtehaj was easily the most relentless advocate of an Iranian market economy, a viable middle class, a capitalist class sure of its investments, and democracy as a smithy wherein these forces could best interact and form.

In his letter, Ebtehaj offered ten reasons why the proposed land reform was detrimental to Iran's long-term capitalist and democratic development. Under a "capitalist system of free enterprise," he wrote in his letter from prison, "it is not right and just that a person may own any number of factories . . . but [be] denied the right to own more than a certain amount of farm land." He agreed that absentee landlordism was a curse and a problem for Iranian agriculture and the economy, but he suggested searching for ways to overcome "the drawbacks . . . without resorting to sequestration." Instead of confiscating property, he offered a "land reform brought about through a system of taxation, where farms would be taxed, based not on actual but optimum yields." He proposed a simple but sophisticated system of taxation that would ultimately bring about the desired changes in the country's agricultural system without undermining the idea of private property.[28]

Ebtehaj's critique is particularly important in its contrast with the Shah's willingness, indeed eagerness, to use the discourse of revolution and the practice of forced sequestration to promote his own political ends and his vision of development. Before long, the Shah would begin to talk incessantly of the White Revolution, and all manner of "sequestration" became part and parcel of the different principles of his revolution. The Shah had a pseudo-socialist, "statist" vision of the economy wherein the state could and should become an economic leviathan. As Ebtehaj had predicted, not long after land reform, the Shah proved willing to forcefully expropriate the country's only private television company, the first private university, and the country's richest private mine. By the mid-seventies, industrialists were ordered by royal fiat to give at least fifty percent of their companies' shares of stock to their workers. In the months before the revolution, he used an army of university students who were deputized to punish, even imprison, those who allegedly contributed to inflation. He threatened to use the military to bring down prices.

Both members of the "bazaar"—the traditional heart of trade in Iran and a source of support for the clerical and democratic opposition—and members of the modern industrialist class were disgruntled with these erratic economic policies, subject to the whims of a single man and changeable overnight by royal decrees. A speech to the senate by Gassem Lajevardi, a scion of one of the most important industrialist families in Iran at the time, embodied this disgruntlement. Lajevardi discreetly demanded more stability and accountability in economic policies, asserting that such stability was the only way to guarantee and thus encourage long-term investment.

The speech was important from a different perspective. There was an unwritten contract between the Shah and Iran's entrepreneurial class, particularly those from the ranks of the modern sector. The entrepreneurs would not engage in politics and would accept the Shah's absolute leadership in return for pro-business policies by the government. For two decades, buoyed by rising oil prices, the covenant worked. Iran witnessed impressive socio-economic growth. In fact, it was among the fastest growing developing economies in the world. But the covenant came back to haunt the regime and the entrepreneurial class when the system went into crisis. The entrepreneurs in 1978 were either critical of the Shah or politically impotent and unable to successfully defend the regime or their own investments. Did the Shah's constant conjuring of revolutionary rhetoric make the idea of revolution an accepted part of Iranian political discourse? Did the implicit covenant with the private sector undermine their ability or their resolve to come to the Shah's defense when his regime went into a crisis in 1978? How much did these grandiose promises—e.g., of a rising standard of living, of surpassing Germany and Japan—fuel the population's rising expectations and contribute to the classical J-Curve, of expectations rising faster than the government's ability to satisfy them? In other societies, the word "revolution" brings to mind cataclysmic changes. By 1978, the word had been a constant part of Iran's political vocabulary for almost two decades. By then, the idea of expropriating the assets of successful businessmen had almost become "normal." When, in the months after the revolution, the regime confiscated the properties of fifty-two of Iran's largest industrialist families, the decision caused but a ripple in the media. The idea of the state confiscating a family's private property had not been a novelty for a long time.

At the same time, it was a measure of the Shah's resilience as a politician that, in spite of the great chasm that separated his vision from the policy pushed by the United States since 1959, he not only stayed a close ally of the United States for the next seventeen years but also forced even the Kennedy administration to rethink some key elements of its policy. At the end of a state visit to the United States in 1962, in a joint press conference with the Shah, Kennedy insisted that "a modern political leader" must work "not just with the upper elements of society" but also "with the ordinary mass of people." The Shah in return accepted the premise but added that "firm action is necessary and he was sure that the United States would not insist on absolute constitutional legality within Iran." Kennedy responded by accepting that "special situations" sometimes exist in different countries and that in Iran "the Shah was the keystone of . . . security and progress."[29] Diplomats who had met with the Shah both before and after this trip reported that his despondent, anxious mood before departure changed to one of buoyancy and self-confidence after his return from America.

The irony is that ultimately the Shah's success in defying U.S. pressure for democratization proved to be his undoing. Had the Shah remained a constitutional monarch, as American policy had proposed during much of the Shah's reign, instead of becoming a modernizing but authoritarian monarch, as the Shah became in the seventies, he might have been able to save his throne and the monarchy. As early as 1975, Richard Helms, one-time head of the CIA and then U.S. ambassador to Iran, wrote in his end-of-tour report, "The conflict between rapid economic growth and modernization

vis-à-vis a still autocratic rule . . . is the greatest uncertainty
of Iranian politics." Helms went on to say that "alas, history
provides discouraging precedents" for a peaceful resolution of
this conflict. "I can recall no example of a ruler willingly
loosening the reins of power."[30] By the time the Shah was
willing to make some democratic concessions, he was already
deemed too vulnerable and weak by his opponents. By then,
Khomeini had emerged as the leader of the opposition and
he wanted nothing short of an end to the monarchy itself.

During the height of his days of power, the Shah had
followed a scorched-earth political policy, making it impossible for the moderate opposition to survive; the only group
that was allowed to organize was the clergy. In every city and
town, every village and neighborhood, there was a mosque.
The Shah allowed them to exist, indeed encouraged them to
grow, in the belief that they would prove a bulwark against
the Left, who remained in his mind the main threat to his
regime. All genuine political parties were declared illegal. Instead, the Shah, under pressure by the American government,
willed into existence first a two-party system and then something called the Progressive Circle—this group eventually became a political party (*Iran Novin*, or New Iran). In those
days, a circle of friends—*dowreh*—was a de facto form of
organization. One of the most powerful such *dowrehs* was
formed by graduates of American universities. The entire
group more or less joined the Progressive Circle. The group's
founding members were Hassan Ali Mansur and Amir Abbas
Hoveyda, with the former openly boasting of the support he
enjoyed "from our American friends."

Mansur became prime minister in 1964 but was mur-
dered after a year in office. During his tenure, the parliament
passed a Status of Forces Agreement with the United States;

it was in defiant opposition to this bill that Khomeini was catapulted into the center of Iranian politics. The State Department had been against the idea of demanding a SOFA from Iran, arguing that such a bill smacked of colonialism. But the Defense Department refused to send American advisors to Iran without such an agreement and the Shah personally pressured the parliament to pass the SOFA. When Khomeini continued his opposition to the bill, he was exiled first to Turkey and then to Iraq. In retaliation, his supporters assassinated Mansur. Hoveyda took over the reins of the cabinet and remained prime minister for thirteen years. All his political life, Hoveyda was under attack by the clergy for his alleged Bahai affiliations. In reality, his father was a devout member of the Bahai faith, but neither of the sons—Amir Abbas and Fereydoon—became Bahais. Both were, at best, agnostic in matters of religion. Fereydoon was a prominent intellectual, film critic, and novelist, and a founding member of the famous French film magazine *Cahiers du Cinema*. After the revolution, Fereydoon escaped to the West, where he wrote scathing critical commentaries and books about the clerical regime and the Shah—the latter of whom, in Fereydoon's view, had heartlessly left Amir Abbas in Iran and in prison. The Shah, according to Ambassador William H. Sullivan's memoirs, dismissed Hoveyda only when he thought that the United States was no longer happy with Hoveyda's tenure. When he fell into the hands of the clerical regime, Hoveyda was executed after a summary trial conducted by the infamous "hanging judge" Sadeq Khalkhali. The CIA chief in Tehran, Gratian Yatsevitch, who had played a crucial role in creating and strengthening the Progressive Circle in the early sixties, initially intended it to "take the wind out of the sail" of the National Front and other moderate opposition forces who refused to make peace with the Shah.[31] Sadly, neither Mansur nor Hoveyda proved willing or capable of playing that role, and both ended up executed by Islamic forces.

Once in power, members of the Progressive Circle, particularly Hoveyda, not only made no effort to promote democracy but also became great facilitators of the Shah's increasing authoritarianism. As the price of oil jumped and the social fabric of Iranian society changed with stunning rapidity, increasing the need for a more democratic polity, the Shah became more and more authoritarian. The rapidity of these changes fueled his grandiosity and his belief that he was anointed to defy the age-old dictum that modern middle classes want a share of power. The faux moderates of the Progressive Circle became his sycophantic servants and the real moderates, whether inside the National Front or among the ranks of Iran's burgeoning middle class, eventually joined the opposition.

Iran's economic heyday was a period in which the middle class saw its greatest prosperity but in which millions of peasants, unable to eke out a living from the small pieces of land they had received during land reform, swelled the ranks of the rapidly rising urban masses. It coincided with the Nixon administration and his Nixon Doctrine. The United States faced an apparently intractable enemy in Southeast Asia. U.S. domination of the international financial system, codified in the Bretton Woods agreement of 1944, was being challenged by a resurgent Europe and Japan. The Shah, according to the Nixon Doctrine, was the designated guarantor of security in the Persian Gulf. The U.S. government was ordered to no longer try to limit the Shah's purchase of military hardware— a constant point of contention between the Shah and successive U.S. administrations—nor to continue to pressure him for more political liberalization. But in reality, even the Nixon Doctrine has a history different from the cold war narrative offered by the Soviets and the Iranian clerics or leftists.

Since 1965, when the Shah first learned of Britain's plans to leave its bases in the Persian Gulf, the Shah insisted that Iran must replace it as the hegemonic force in the region. Britain was opposed to this idea but Nixon had close ties to the Shah and had been particularly impressed when both he and Ardeshir Zahedi, one-time ambassador to the United States, continued their support of Nixon even after his defeat in California's gubernatorial campaign. When he travelled to Iran in 1966, at a time when he was truly in the political wilderness, Nixon met with the Shah for four hours and was impressed with his ideas about turning Iran into the police-man of the Persian Gulf. Those were the days of the Vietnam War, and the United States believed its forces were over-extended around the world. Economic pressures emanating from a slowdown in the U.S. economy and French President Charles de Gaulle's threat to cash in his share of Eurodollars and demand gold for them—as promised in the Bretton Woods agreement—made the Shah's ideas more appealing to Nixon. In Tehran in 1966 then, the idea of the Nixon Doctrine began to germinate.

Two primary examples of how the Nixon Doctrine worked in these years can be found in the cases of Dhofar and Iraqi Kurdistan. In the early seventies, in the feudal kingdom of Oman on the Arabian Peninsula, there was a communist movement based in the province of Dhofar that received assistance from both China and the Soviet Union. This armed insurgency came to control a sizeable portion of the country, leading to a threat that the crucial waterway of the Strait of Hormuz would be literally under the communist gun. The Shah secretly sent in Iranian forces, which (aided by small forces from Great Britain, Jordan, and other countries) successfully defeated the communist insurgency. Absent the Iranian military, either U.S. or British forces would have had to take up the challenge.

In Iraq, too, the Nixon Doctrine and the Shah's new sense of empowerment and hegemony had unanticipated consequences. After the new Ba'ath regime came to power in 1968, it openly flirted with the Soviet Union. The Russians were using their influence in the Iraqi communist party and in some of the Kurdish circles in Iraq to try to create a new alliance between the Ba'ath and these opposition parties. The Shah worried that such an alliance would create a Soviet foothold in Iraq, thus providing a first step toward domination of the Persian Gulf. He convinced the Nixon administration and the Israeli government to commence a joint operation, implemented by Iran, wherein Iraqi Kurds were armed and aided to become a nuisance for the new Iraqi government. This covert operation channeled millions of dollars to Iraqi Kurds fighting the Ba'ath regime. It ended only in 1975, with no warning to the Iraqi Kurdish parties, when the Shah suddenly decided to sign an agreement with Saddam Hussein, by then the strongman of Iraqi politics.

As the Nixon administration decided to cease all pressure on the Shah to limit his military budget and as American pressure for democratization all but disappeared, the Shah, buoyed by his victories in increasing the price of oil, became more and more authoritarian. Prudent moderates, advocating reform and democracy, as well as radical advocates of change from every political persuasion, were shunned and barred from politics. The Shah believed that the clergy—with the exception of a few Khomeini supporters—were his reliable

allies in the fight against both communists and secular nationalists. His scorched-earth policy gave the clergy and their
vast, nimble network of organizations an opportunity to grow
and to monopolize the public domain. When, in October
1969, moderate religious leaders sent a message to the Shah
and to the U.S. embassy that they were worried about the
situation in the country and angry at Khomeini for putting
them in the difficult position of choosing his radicalism or
being branded reactionary mullahs, the Shah and the embassy
both chose to ignore their warnings. More than once, the
Shah ignored similar warnings from the moderate clergy
about everything from the Shah's sudden decision to change
the calendar and make it a "royal" rather than Islamic calendar, to new laws about women and family protection.

The more the Shah and the American embassy ignored
the moderate clergy, the easier it became for Khomeini and
his radical allies to gain and consolidate hegemony over religious forces in Iran.[32] As a result, when the regime went into
a crisis in 1977, the clerical network, soon dominated by
Khomeini, turned out to be the only force capable of offering
itself as a viable alternative to the Shah. By promoting economic changes that created a new, wealthier, educated middle
class, the Shah inadvertently created the forces necessary for
a democratic transition. The millions of peasants who had
converged on the cities as a result of the land reform became
the foot soldiers of this revolution. His scorched-earth political policy, however, denied these forces either a share of
power or an opportunity to organize within the limits clearly
set out by the constitution. When, in December 1978,
George Ball concluded that the United States should urgently
seek "to open a disavowable (sic) channel of communication"
with the opposition, it had no choice but to negotiate with

Khomeini and his entourage.[33] Iran's fledgling democratic opposition was in a similar bind. Its alliance with Khomeini was
indeed a marriage of strange bedfellows, but it was in many
ways the unavoidable consequence of the Shah's contradictory
policies.

What made the work of the opposition easier was the
Shah's sudden decision to scuttle the two-part party system
he had created under American pressure and instead create a
new one-party system. Called Resurgence, the party was a
stillborn monster and an immediate source of discontent, even
ridicule. The fact that key party ideologues were from the
ranks of lapsed Stalinists made the organization behave like a
pseudo-Stalinist monstrosity of bad ideas and even worse politics. Some think the idea came to the Shah from Sadat in
Egypt. Others point the finger at a group of five mostly Amer-
ican-trained technocrats who suggested the one-party system
based on American political scientist Samuel Huntington's
prescription for political development in developing countries.
Whatever the source, the idea was a political liability and
added to the already brewing sense of discontent. Even then,
in spite of the Shah's newfound independence and numerous
public arguments with the United States over the price of oil,
the opposition still succeeded in labeling him a "lackey of the
United States" and blaming the United States for his policies.

By then, the Shah was full of grandiose ideas about his
own wisdom and about the political and economic poverty
of the West, particularly America. More than once he lashed
out against the frailties and faults of liberal democracy. The
fact that many American politicians joined their Iranian counterparts to pile sycophantic praise on the Shah only added to
his belief in his own divine destiny. Of these sycophants, none
could match Nelson Rockefeller, who compared the Shah to

Alexander the Great and added wistfully that "we must take His Majesty to the U.S. for a couple of years so that he can teach us how to run a country."[34]

Not long after the creation of the Resurgence Party, the Carter administration came to power. Jimmy Carter broke with the Nixon realpolitik and strongly espoused the idea that American allies like the Shah should show more genuine respect for human rights. Moreover, in the last years of the Nixon administration and through much of the Ford administration, Iran and the United States were fighting a quiet war of diplomacy over the price of oil. Eventually, the United States made a covert pact with Saudi Arabia to bring down the price. Some scholars have even claimed that the drop in the price of oil precipitated the fall of the Shah. Just as Iran's revenues were drastically reduced with the falling price of oil, the Carter administration put pressure on the Shah to democratize and liberalize. The timing could not have been worse: the Shah was sick and the economy was in a downturn. The normal instabilities that accompany any authoritarian regime's attempt to democratize only augmented the destabilizing effects of the economic crisis. By 1978, Iran's GNP growth in real terms dropped to 2.8 percent. This recessionary slowdown was exacerbated by unusually high inflationary rates caused by reckless government expenditures. Like much of the West, Iran faced the strange hybrid phenomenon of "stagflation." Some in the U.S. Congress began to worry about Iran's budgetary priorities (and the fact that, in line with the Shah's views, precedence was given to military matters over social needs). These anxieties led to the idea of "linking Iran's human rights performance with arms transfer."[35] It is hard not to wonder what might have happened in Iran had Congress developed such a matrix a decade earlier, when Nixon was giving the Shah carte blanche to buy any non-nuclear weapons system he desired. But in 1978, such a matrix was just one more indication to the Iranian opposition that the Shah's position was precarious and vulnerable in America, deemed by many as the omnipotent force in Iran. As Montazeri, second only to Khomeini in the early days of the Islamic revolution, wrote in his memoirs, Carter's human rights policies were in no small measure responsible for the resurgence of opposition to the Shah and the victory of the Islamic revolution. Many other memoirs from the same period reaffirm this claim about the role of U.S. policy in unleashing a dormant democratic opposition. The Shah's deteriorating emotional and physical condition combined with these other factors to create the perfect storm that was the revolution.

The Soviet Union was watching these developments rather closely. In the Shah's problems, they saw opportunity. Their handmaiden, the Tudeh Party, eager to become the legal and loyal opposition to the Shah in the mid-sixties— right after the Shah had signed an economic deal with the Soviet Union—suddenly became more militant in its criticism of him. In the months leading up to the 1979 revolution, the Shah's cold war fears were augmented by a series of events that convinced him that the Soviet Union was out to overthrow him. In 1977, the Iranian secret police (SAVAK) arrested a two-star general who had been, for almost three decades, a paid agent of the KGB. For much of his political life, the Shah had had an exaggerated view of the KGB's power in Iran. The arrest of Ahmad Mogharebi only exacerbated these fears. Events in 1978 caused even greater dread in both the Shah and the U.S. government.

On November 19, 1978, Soviet leader Leonid Brezhnev threatened an invasion of Iran if "anti-Soviet" elements were to gain the upper hand in the country. The statement was, in short order, followed by a confidential letter from Brezhnev to President Carter "suggesting that because the Soviets have a long border with Iran, they should enjoy a special position of influence."[36] Ever since 1917, Soviet leaders had tried to turn Iran into another Finland, where "anti-Soviet activities" constantly threatened to trigger a Russian invasion. They used Article Six of the 1921 Soviet-Iran agreement—or, more accurately, their self-serving interpretation of that article—as the legal basis for their attempted "Finlandization." Iran had initially agreed to the article only in the context of the tumultuous situation in the years following the 1917 revolution. The article in fact allowed Soviet intervention only if White Russian forces used Iran as a base of attack on the newly established Bolshevik government. But in subsequent years, the Soviets had their own "expanded" interpretation of the article and used it many times to threaten an attack. The 1978 Brezhnev letter to Carter was only the latest example of this tactic.

Moreover, leaders of the Soviet-backed Tudeh Party who had been living in Eastern Europe or the Soviet Union for three decades were returning to Iran in 1978, reviving the old party apparatus. From the first moment of their arrival, the party leaders supported Khomeini and the most anti-democratic, anti-American wings within the clergy and the rest of the opposition. The party used its extensive propaganda apparatus to promote anti-American and anti-democratic slogans.

Carter's human rights policies convinced the Shah to release almost all of Iran's four thousand political prisoners. Nearly every one of these newly released prisoners had long experience in underground organizational techniques. Dozens had been trained by radical Palestinian groups and knew the methods of terrorism—romanticized in those days of Fanon and his "apotheosis of violence" as the admired art of urban guerrilla warfare. The prisoners' release strengthened the opposition and weakened the resolve of the regime and SAVAK, but also weakened the prospects of democracy in Iran. Most of these recently released prisoners were schooled in Stalinist models of Marxism and dismissed liberal democracy as a "frivolous" and "fraudulent" bourgeois gimmick. Even forces loyal to the Mojahedeen-e Khalg-e Iran (MEK), though ostensibly following an Islamic ideology, were in fact supporting an eclectic mix of Leninism and their own version of Islamic "liberation theology."[37] The handful of clerics in prison at the time—from Ayatollah Montazeri and Mahmoud Taleghani to Ali Akbar Hashemi Rafsanjani—were also freed and invariably joined the ranks of Khomeini supporters. Nothing united these disparate forces as much as their shared opposition to "imperialism," particularly that of the United States.

Another factor was the Confederation of Iranian Students, created as the result of the arrival of thousands of Iranian students in some of the top European and American universities. Until then, educational sojourns to the West had been a privilege limited to the children of the elite. But indispensable to the Shah's modernization plans was a large, trained technocratic class, and Iran lacked the educational infrastructure to train such a class. Sociologists have called the late fifties the age of the technocrats, and American policy in Iran strongly advocated that new young technocrats must gradually take the place of traditional politicians. Starting in the late fifties, inexpensive bus, train, and eventually plane service from Iran to Europe and America became available and students from all social classes began to arrive in the West. The

Shah made the mistake Russian czars made in the late nineteenth century. Hoping to avoid the "dangerous" ideas of the French Revolution, czars insisted on sending their students to Prussia, where they learned Marxism. The Shah saw Marxism as his main enemy, and thus insisted on sending Iranian students to democratic Europe and America. The more radical elements used their newfound freedom in Western democracies to create the Confederation of Iranian Students—an international organization that became a formidable foe of the Shah throughout the sixties and seventies. Instead of liberal democracy and the market economy, these students were enamored of new and old Leftist ideas. Che Guevara and Mao Tse-tung, not Jefferson and John Stuart Mill, were their champions.

In the seventies, the Confederation became a powerful source of propaganda against the Shah, advocating for either Khomeini or yet another "proletarian revolution." Dominated by the Left and structured along the lines of the "United Front" suggested by Stalin in the thirties—communists leading the largest number of democratic forces in a common battle—the Confederation of Iranian Students was instrumental in turning the students' democratic aspirations into a force for radicalism, highly critical of the United States. As the Shah's regime showed incipient signs of collapse, leaders of the Confederation returned to Iran. There they joined forces with Khomeini supporters and, united by their anti-Americanism, advocated not a democratic transition but a radical revolution. Before long, at least two hundred members of the Confederation were executed by the new Islamic regime's firing squads. The student movements' Leftist tendencies and Khomeini's ability to pitch his ideas in a language that made them part of the "anti-imperialist discourse" made it easier for this strange alliance of modernizing students and a de-modernizing clergy to exist.

An unfortunate romance developed—and continues to exist to some degree today—between Leftist Iranian intellectuals and the clerical regime that came to power in Iran. Some of the most renowned Western intellectuals also fell prey to this strange romance. The regime's egregious breaches of democratic rights were often overlooked by these Western Leftists because of its alleged "struggle against imperialism." French historian Michel Foucault's brief infatuation with Khomeini as the embodiment of a radically new "critique of modernity" is arguably the most risible and tragic example of this romantic folly.[38]

At the same time, the Confederation was a constant source of tension between the Shah and the United States. From the organization's first days, when activists like Sadeq Qotb-Zadeh lived in the United States, its oppositional activity was deemed by the Shah as a sure sign that the CIA and American officials supported the group and meant to use it to undermine his authority. In 1962, for example, the Iranian embassy demanded extradition for Qotb-Zadeh; Attorney General Bobby Kennedy refused the request, suggesting that Qotb-Zadeh and other activists were not communists, as claimed by the Shah, but nationalists demanding democratic change in their country. The visa status of Confederation activists in the United States remained a source of tension between the Shah and the United States for much of the sixties and seventies. The Shah's government tried to get these students extradited by having the Iranian embassy refuse to renew their passports. Without a valid passport, Iran assumed, the United States could not renew the students' visas and must throw them out of the country. The Kennedy administration successfully pushed for passage of a special law that allowed the United States to renew the visas of Iranian students whose passports had not been renewed by the Iranian embassy in the United States. The Shah and his royalist supporters considered this unusual exception, allowed for critics of a dependable ally of America, as a sure sign that America was in collusion with the opposition.

Even this unusual constellation of stars was not enough to end the Shah's regime yet. In the last two years of his rule, in each moment of crisis, the Shah arguably made the worst possible choice. He showed weakness when he needed to be strong, and he feigned power when he in fact had none. The reason for this remarkable series of errors was not tactical but strategic, rooted in his view that the revolution was a conspiracy of foreign powers. He sometimes focused his wrath on the United States, other times on oil companies, and always on communists. Compounding the Shah's gross mismanagement and misunderstanding of the crisis was also the Carter administration's gross mishandling of the crisis.

In his last book, *Answer to History*, written long after he had been dethroned, the Shah argued with surprising certainty that the revolution was indeed a conspiracy of oil companies and communists. He argued that to "understand the upheaval in Iran . . . one must understand the politics of oil." He claimed that as soon as he began to insist on a fair share of oil wealth for Iran, "a systematic campaign of denigration was begun concerning my government and my person . . . it was at this time that I became a despot, an oppressor, a tyrant . . . This campaign began in 1958, reached its peak in 1961. Our White Revolution halted it temporarily. But it was begun with greater vigor in 1975 and increased until my departure."[39]

In the critical months leading to the revolution, his fear that the United States was behind the revolution, along with his own insecurities, begot in him an urgent need for signs of support from the United States. Unfortunately, the messages he received from America were contradictory. For example, when the American ambassador, Bill Sullivan, was told by concerned Iranian officials that "a personal message of support for the Shah from President Carter" would go a long way to improve the king's mood and ability to rule, the ambassador rejected the request, "saying that such a message would be unusual and inappropriate [at] the present time."[40] The response depressed the Shah; but a few weeks later, when he was told that he would be in fact "receiving a telephone call" from the president, "the Shah was clearly delighted," and according to Sullivan, "his chin moved from his knees to at least his chest."[41]

In reality, there were profound differences in the messages the Shah was receiving from the White House, the National Security Council, the CIA, and the State Department. For many years, it had become something of a ritual that the CIA station chief in Tehran would regularly meet with the Shah. What he was telling the Shah in the last months of 1978 remains altogether a mystery. The stark difference between directives from the State Department and the National Security Council created a vacuum wherein Sullivan seemed to have followed his own "foreign policy." While Brzezinski, Carter's national security advisor, supported an "iron fist policy" to establish law and order, followed by concessions to the opposition, the State Department insisted on the continuation of the liberalization policy. The Shah, caught between these conflicting words of advice, by disposition indecisive in times of crisis, and weakened by the onset of cancer, swung from one extreme to another, invariably to disastrous results. On the other hand, Khomeini, dangling a tactical but tantalizing democratic platform, used each of the Shah's moves to his own benefit.

Of the many problems plaguing U.S.-Iranian relations in the last thirty years, the most elemental problem is the one most easily overlooked or ignored: the United States plays by the normal rules and logic of diplomacy while the clerical regime plays by its own idiosyncratic rules. Trying to deal with the regime only through traditional channels of diplomacy is akin to fighting an agile terrorist insurgency with the ponderous might of a regular army. While it is clear that there is no military solution to America's "Iran problem," it is no less clear that a new paradigm, equipped to counter the Iranian regime's self-serving rules of conduct, needs to be developed. The Iranian regime's agility is rooted in its despotism; the ponderous pace of American policy is the price society pays for democracy. The challenge is to match Iran's agility without sacrificing the principles of democracy.

In the last three decades, the history of U.S. relations with Iran has been the history of an asymmetrical diplomatic, military, and economic confrontation. Every year the clerical regime has sent hundreds of its trusted intelligence and IRGC officers to train in Western universities, particularly those in England and Canada. They return home with some knowledge of the inevitable tensions that exist within democratic societies and they use this knowledge to better navigate their way around U.S. foreign policy. At the same time, in America, the bitterness of the 1979 hostage crisis seems to have been the culprit in reversing a long-held tradition of making ample public funding available to study the culture and society of a nation that promises to pose a challenge. Though successive

administrations have referred to Iran as the greatest challenge
facing America, before September 11, 2001, the number of
centers and programs studying Iran in fact diminished in this
country. Along with the fact that the United States has no
embassy in Tehran, this dearth of impartial scholarly inquiry
and knowledge has diminished America's effective power by
creating an epistemological knowledge imbalance with the regime. This favors the clerical regime, allowing it to use the
tensions in America, and between America and its allies, to
its own ends. At the same time, the rifts within the Iranian
regime, and between the regime and the people, remain mis-
understood and therefore untapped by the United States. The
knowledge vacuum in Washington has been filled by neo-
phytes and expatriates with political agendas of their own.

The result of this today is a diplomatic disparity between
the regime, with its double talk and outright lies, and the
United States, trying to play by the traditional rules of diplomacy. *Tagiyeh*, a Shiite concept allowing the faithful to lie in
the service of faith, provides clerical leaders with a theological
cover for their lies and obfuscation. Democracy is a system of
checks and balances, of ultimate reckoning, and of a potential
political price for every policy decision. Many careers were
lost or damaged in America as the result of what came to be
known as the Iran-Contra affair. In Iran, it is still not clear
who was involved in the decision to initiate those negotiations. We know that Rafsanjani, Khamenei, and Moussavi
were involved behind the scenes but never participated directly in the negotiations. The regime has kept a pragmatic
silence on this. None of the leaders paid any price for any
role they might have played in the episode. Only in recent
months, Rafsanjani and Moussavi have come under attack for
their "soft" approach to the United States. In fact, the only

person who paid a price (with his life) was a staffer in Ayatollah Montazeri's office, who leaked to a Lebanese paper the story of the regime's hypocrisy, engaging in its rhetorical anti-American and anti-Israeli flourishes while at the same time secretly dealing with both countries. When Montazeri—at the time the designated successor to Khomeini, and ostensibly the second man in the political hierarchy—asked Rafsanjani, then speaker of the Majlis, why he and his allies had decided to enter into these covert and startling negotiations, the only response he got was, "How did you find out about the negotiations?"

The most obvious aspect of this asymmetry has been in the military domain, where the clerical regime has found it convenient to help insurgents in places like Iraq, Afghanistan, Lebanon, and Yemen to challenge either the United States or its proxies. The message the regime has tried to send to the United States and Israel has been simple, though not necessarily credible: attack Iran and you will be attacked by Iran's proxies and clients. The two reported examples of the United States trying to conduct a similar asymmetrical war involve support for the Pakistani group, Jondollah, and an effort to maintain the Mojahedeen-e Khalg-e Iran in Iraq, and use them as foot soldiers in such a battle. Created in the mid-sixties, the MEK combined elements of radical Marxism with its own interpretation of Shiism. MEK leaders were Shiism's "liberation theology" proponents, with the added component of terrorist activities. In the early eighties, they engaged in an effective but bloody terrorist war with the regime, wherein thousands of their members and hundreds of regime officials lost their lives. In the years before the revolution, MEK had also assassinated a number of American citizens working in Iran, making it a hard sell in this country. Nonetheless, the fact that MEK had worked with Saddam Hussein against Iran and engaged in brutal acts of terrorism in its early days made America's support for it a propaganda bonanza for the clerical regime in Tehran.

The economic asymmetry between the two countries has been caused by several factors. The regime uses thousands of front companies and holding companies, as well as criminally greedy individuals, to conduct its business around the world. It uses everything from the traditional system of *havaleh*— where millions of dollars are transferred across national boundaries with absolutely no paper trace and none of the normal forms of financial transfer—to these dummy companies to conduct some of its most nefarious financial transactions. Traditional financial forensics can only go halfway in unraveling the intricate web of institutions and transactions used by the regime. The reported discovery of billions of dollars worth of hundred-dollar bills and gold bullion in a truck on the Turkish border, and the existence of one account with more than a billion dollars in it in the name of Mojtaba, one of Khamenei's sons, are only a few examples of these financial shenanigans.

Moreover, the greed of corporations—many in Europe and a handful in America—has helped the Iranian regime bypass the intended pressures of the American-U.N. embargo. While American corporations lost a market worth billions of dollars, their competitors walked away with windfall profits. The regime in Iran used the embargo not only as an excuse for its own incompetence but as fodder for its continued anti-Americanism. Chinese, Russian, and Indian companies have further enabled the regime to counter the effects of the embargo.

But long before there was any talk of an embargo, the

clerical regime had cleverly managed to create a crucial asymmetry in its relations with the United States. The use of the myth of the Great Satan put the United States in a defensive mode from the beginning.

The Carter administration had, although inadvertently, aided in the success of the Islamic revolution. And in January 1979, in a still unpublished letter, Khomeini wrote to Carter promising a peaceful transition of power if the United States discontinued its support for the Shah and Bakhtiyar, the last prime minister. Once in power, however, Khomeini began to use anti-Americanism as a major tool of hegemony, both domestically and among the Muslims of the world.

In the months after the fall of the Shah, the Carter administration went out of its way to maintain cordial (if not close) relations with the new regime. It signaled willingness to respect all past agreements between the two nations and even rescinded the offer of safe sanctuary it earlier made to the Shah and his family before they left Iran. Bringing the Shah to the United States, officials now told Carter, would jeopardize U.S. diplomats and interests. Before becoming seriously sick, the Shah had confided to the British government that he had no desire to settle in the United States. He said he disliked "the American way of life" and was particularly embittered by what he considered America's key role in the collapse of his regime. And thus the Shah became, in the words of Henry Kissinger, "the flying Dutchman."

After several months of humiliating wandering around the world, when the Shah was shunned by virtually every country except Sadat's Egypt, the Shah's health deteriorated. His physicians recommended that he be allowed into the United States for an urgently needed medical operation. The Carter administration for a while rejected this request. But many prominent Americans, from David Rockefeller and Henry Kissinger to Richard Nixon and Senator Charles Percy, pressured Carter to change his mind and admit the Shah on humanitarian grounds. Before making the final decision, Carter went out of his way to reassure the Iranian regime that admitting the Shah had no political connotation and there were no plans "to repeat the events of August 1953." He assured the Iranian regime that the Shah's stay in the United States would be temporary and only for medical purposes, and that he and his family would be barred from any political activity. The Iranian regime went so far as to demand that a physician of its choosing should examine the Shah and confirm the seriousness of his condition. The United States responded by indicating that an independent, trusted team of American physicians had in fact examined the Shah and confirmed the urgent need for an operation.

This extraordinary attempt to accommodate the new revolutionary regime in Tehran was anything but reciprocal. Every day in the Iranian press some new "dirty secret" of U.S. involvement in Iran was exposed. The pro-Soviet Marxists used their influence in the media and the cultural domain to offer some theoretical varnish to this clerical xenophobia. One day it was the picture of the now-empty bunkers used by U.S. intelligence officers to house their anti-Soviet listening centers. The next day it was another revelation about America's nefarious ties with the Shah and his dreaded secret police. Although the clergy, particularly Khomeini's one-time mentor, Mostafa Kashani, had played a key role in the fall of Mossadeq by joining royalist forces in 1953, there was no end to Islamic regime recitations about America's "original sin" in the overthrow of the Mossadeq government.

The fact that the Shah had built a strong army using

mostly American weapons and planes was another often-cited American sin. The fact that innumerable archival documents show clearly that for much of the post-war years the United States tried to temper the Shah's grandiose military plans was conveniently overlooked. Even later, when the same much-maligned arsenal proved indispensable in fighting Iraq's attack, there was no change in the vehemence of the rhetoric against America's "military-industrial complex." In fact, the United States was directly blamed for the Iraqi invasion of Iran. Without an American green light, the whisper went, Saddam would have never dared attack Iran. Other conveniently forgotten truths include the fact that Khomeini had, weeks before the Iraqi invasion, executed about half of Iran's air force officer corps on the charge of alleged conspiracy in a coup attempt—a coup that was apparently first "reported" by members of the Tudeh Party; that he continued to incite Iraqi Shiites to revolt against Saddam; and that many members of Iran's opposition told Saddam and the United States that Khomeini's regime was about to fall and disgruntled Iranians would welcome an Iraqi invasion. Blaming America was the most convenient "explanation" of a destructive war that was begun by two men's megalomania and continued needlessly because of Khomeini's desire to end Saddam's rule in Iraq.

Lamentable aspects of U.S. policy in this period helped the regime in its propaganda. The decision by the Reagan administration to publicly side with Iraq, and even provide it with intelligence on Iranian military plans, while at the same time covertly selling airplane parts and missiles to Iran in the Iran-Contra Affair, provided Khomeini and his successor all the ammunition they needed to continue their anti-Americanism. Another U.S. blunder came when Saddam Hussein used chemical weapons against Iranian soldiers and civilians and the United States did little to condemn this egregious act. In fact, America's ominous silence about the Iraqi use of chemical weapons—despite the opposition to this silence by figures like Secretary of State George Shultz—had an important, albeit unintended, consequence of lasting impact.

Among America's sins, in the eyes of Khomeini, was its help in the development of a nuclear program for Iran. It had all begun with Eisenhower's Atoms for Peace in 1959 and the gift of a small research reactor for Tehran University. In fact, for a decade, all but nothing was done with the reactor. Iran's nuclear program began in earnest only in the early seventies, when Iran was flush with cash and the Shah increasingly saw himself as a world leader. By then, having a nuclear program had become, in his mind, the *sine qua non* of progress and prominence. With little advance planning and no public discussion, he ordered the commencement of a $2-billion-a-year nuclear program. The United States, European nuclear powers, Israel, and South Africa were all active proponents of Iran's nuclear program. Companies competed ferociously for the chance to be part of Iran's nuclear future. By the time of the revolution, a partially completed nuclear reactor in the city of Bushehr, a number of contracts with companies around the world, and hundreds of Iranian students studying nuclear physics at the best universities around the world were the only tangible result of this program.

As Khomeini never tired of repeating, the Shah was a "lackey" of the United States and it was the master's order that Iran should buy "this useless nuclear junk." Khomeini ordered the suspension of all work on the program. Even the Bushehr nuclear plant, in spite of Iran's investment of billions of dollars toward its completion, was suspended. Use it as a silo to store wheat, Khomeini reportedly ordered.

He changed his mind in less than five years, when the world did nothing to condemn Saddam's criminal use of chemical weapons against Iranians. The nuclear program was commenced, but this time covertly. In 1991, when Iran's secret program was finally exposed, the regime claimed it had chosen the covert path because it worried about an Israeli or American attack on Iranian nuclear sites. In the words of Hassan Rouhani, for many years Iran's lead negotiator in nuclear talks with Europe and the International Atomic Energy Agency, Iran had been trying to "do a North Korea." It wanted the world to face a *fait accompli*. In the four years after Rouhani's 2006 speech was made public, the regime has continued to follow the same strategy and it has, remarkably, succeeded in befuddling the world. When the speech was made, Iran had only a hundred fifty centrifuges running. Today it has more than seven thousand. In February 2010, the regime announced that it intends to enrich uranium up to twenty percent. In a report issued by IAEA soon after this announcement, the organization indicated its "concern" about the regime's nuclear plans and its work on missiles capable of carrying nuclear warheads.

It was of course not just guile and duplicity or clever double talk that allowed the regime to succeed in its strategy even after the world knew what it was attempting to do. In its efforts it was helped by the newly assertive foreign policy of Russia and China and by the greed of many European countries and companies. The latter continued to do business with the clerical regime even after it was found to be in violation of its Nuclear Non-Proliferation Treaty (NPT) obligations and after the United Nations had imposed sanctions as punishment.

In the pursuit of its nuclear strategy, the regime played another card successfully. It accused the United States of hypocrisy and of arbitrarily picking on Iran. The United States, according to this narrative, had encouraged the Shah to have up to twenty nuclear reactors; yet now that the Islamic revolutionary regime was in power, the United States was arbitrarily barring Iran from exercising its rights under the NPT. But as with so much else in the regime's self-serving narrative of history, the United States' initial encouragement of the Shah is the only kernel of truth in this story. In fact, as soon as the United States learned of the Shah's unusually heavy investment in uranium enrichment activities in Iran and around the world—particularly South Africa and France—it tried vigorously to dissuade the Shah from pursuing that path. By then there were signs that Iran was pursuing dual-use technologies that could potentially be used in the development of a nuclear bomb. The Shah wanted to have the technological know-how to develop the bomb as soon as "anyone in the neighborhood" went nuclear. The Ford and Carter administrations made every effort to dissuade the Shah from this trajectory. Surprisingly, successive U.S. administrations have allowed the Iranian regime to maintain its lie, whereas recently declassified documents from the State Department, Defense Department, White House, and Department of Energy show the details of tense and sometimes rancorous negotiations between the Shah and the United States over the wisdom of Iran's enrichment activities.

CHAPTER FOUR

Flirting with Disaster
The United States, Iran,
and the "Eastern Look"

Desperate times often beget desperate measures. For the Iranian regime, desperate times have arrived as a result of its continued confrontation with the United States, the accumulating economic woes brought about by its incompetence, corruption, and mismanagement, and the falling price of oil, compounded by the increasingly sharp bite of U.N. sanctions. In response to these crises—and in an attempt to solve the problem of America's relentless pressure vis-à-vis human rights and democracy in Iran—a powerful faction within the clerical regime has been toying with a geo-strategic shift of tectonic proportions, one that, if realized, would have far-reaching consequences not just for Iran and the United States but for the world.

In recent months, the Iranian media have paid scant attention to the possibility of this shift. Outside Iran, only a handful of scholars and analysts have shown any interest in developments such as Iran's increased trade with China and Russia or in the regime's flirtation with the so-called China Model. This China Model entails economic liberalization and improvement in people's livelihoods in return for continued rule of the Communist Party (or other absolutist ruler). It operates on the axiom of Dostoyevsky's Grand Inquisitor that men and women eagerly bargain away their freedom in return for freedom from want and choice.

Increased trade with authoritarian allies and the lure of this China Model are certainly important issues, but they are only aspects of the far more important paradigmatic shift— one known to its advocates as the "Eastern Look."

A number of factors account for the surprising silence on the subject of this Eastern Look. In the first place, during Ahmadinejad's first term of office (2005–09), as elements of the newly proposed Eastern Look began to unfold, the world was either obsessively preoccupied with Iran's ominous nuclear program or morbidly fascinated by Ahmadinejad's outrageous comments questioning the historical veracity of the Holocaust or the right of the state of Israel to exist. Second, this strategic Eastern Look shares some elements with the Islamic Republic's tactical moves in increasing trade with Asian countries, particularly China, Russia, and India. Every faction within the highly fractured Iranian regime has supported this trade increase, from the "pragmatist" Rafsanjani and the reformist Khatami to the conservative Ali Akbar Asgaroladi, leader of the powerful Mo'talefeh Party. This group and its name were both creations of Khomeini. In 1961–62, as he prepared to challenge the Shah, Khomeini called together the leaders of disparate Islamist groups, several of them terrorists, and ordered them to unite. The group was instrumental in the June 1963 uprising and later in the assassination of Prime Minister Mansur. Ever since 1979, members of Mo'talefeh have invariably been partners in power, showing particular preference for positions that enrich them. They have established intimate ties with the bazaar and the IRGC.

Over the last three years, as U.N. sanctions and U.S. financial pressures have further squeezed the already ailing Ira-

nian economy, a radical minority in Tehran led by Ahmadinejad has used this tactical unity to surreptitiously push ahead
its own design. This calls for a far more radical shift away
from Iran's twenty-five-hundred-year-old westward orientation and toward the Eastern Look. The nuclear program has
been a disastrously costly project, intended solely for the regime's self-preservation; the Eastern Look is potentially an
even more consequential measure, calculated to maintain the
regime in power while ridding it of the constant badgering
by the United States regarding democracy and human rights.
For its advocates, the Eastern Look is the hopeful panacea for
both the regime's domestic problems and its continuous tensions with the United States.

Among countries with assigned roles in the Eastern Look,
China, Russia, India, Pakistan, North and South Korea, Japan, and Malaysia are the most important. As a concept, the
Eastern Look has already entered the Iranian political lexicon.
In 2008, the Islamic regime's foreign ministry organized a
conference to discuss the costs and benefits of such a shift; it
has even published a book on the subject. If realized, the
Eastern Look would beget a realignment in the geo-strategic
balance of power in the Middle East that would have as profound an effect as the Iranian regime getting its hands on a
nuclear weapon.

Iran's nuclear program is one of the biggest challenges
facing President Obama. His administration is clearly aware
that a solution to the Iranian nuclear problem will come not
through preemptive unilateralism but through international
consultation and cooperation. The Obama administration
seems to have already aborted the construction of a missile
defense shield in Eastern Europe in return for promised Russian cooperation in dissuading Iran from developing a nuclear

bomb. Russia welcomed these concessions but has done little
to help the United States with its Iran problem. Only since
February, when the Iranian regime surprised Russia by announcing that it would enrich uranium to twenty percent and
the IAEA in its February 18, 2010 Board of Governors Report
indicated its concern with Iran's intention, has Russia moved,
ever gingerly, away from the regime and closer to the international community. There are even some indications that
there are differences between an increasingly assertive President Dmitry Medvedev and the ever-aggressive Prime Minister Vladimir Putin on the subject of Russian policy on
Iran—the former advocating more cooperation with the West
and the latter repeatedly insisting that there is no "smoking
gun" in Iran's nuclear program to warrant serious international concern or pressure.

The recklessness of those advocating the Eastern Look
paradigm in Iran became evident in late 2008 when whispers
of an impending American or Israeli assault on the country's
nuclear sites reached fever pitch. At that time, a top IRGC
commander cautioned that Iran, if attacked or unduly pressured, would respond by offering China a naval base at the
tip of the Strait of Hormuz—the gateway to the Persian Gulf
often referred to as the energy lifeline for much of Europe,
Japan, and, increasingly, even the United States. While it is
hard to imagine Western powers sitting idly by and allowing
the establishment of such a base, it is equally important to
understand the impolitic recklessness of these Eastern Look
proponents.

From the time of Herodotus (700 BC), whose *Histories*
chronicled the wars between the Greeks and the old Persian
empire, to the two pivotal political challenges of the last century—the containment of the Soviet Union and the rise of

radical Islam—Iran has held a persistent place in the imagination of the West. This is no marginal country on the periphery of the world.

During this same enormously lengthy period, Iran consistently looked to the West as ally, rival, mentor, or market. During the Safavid era (1501–1736), when the Muslims of the Ottoman Empire invaded Europe, Iran not only refused to join them but opened a second front against the Ottomans. The import of this decision was not lost on the European imagination of the time: Shakespeare talks of a "Persian prince/That won three fields of Sultan Soleyman." In our time, scholars as diverse as Mojtaba Minavi in Iran and the influential Orientalist Bernard Lewis in America have argued that Iran's Western tilt changed the outcome of the East-West wars of the Renaissance period. They believe that Persian power, and the challenge Persia presented to the Ottomans in the mid-sixteenth century, helped stall the Ottoman drive against European Christendom. Additionally, and interestingly, in Iranian mythology, the lands of the East—*Touran*—have invariably been the abode of the enemy.

This westward disposition was politically codified in 1955 when Iran forfeited its nominal neutrality and joined the Baghdad Pact, later called CENTO, becoming in treaty and reality an ally of the West. The Shah was unabashed in his desire to have Iran emulate the West in everything, save democracy. Like the Safavid kings who broke with the Ottoman Muslims, the Shah broke with nearly every Muslim country and formed a de facto alliance with Israel and the West, particularly the United States. Even in the early years of the Islamic Republic, although Iran ended its de facto diplomatic ties with Israel, an Occidental disposition, this time more tempered and critical, still prevailed. At the height of Khomeini's anti-Israeli and anti-Zionist rhetoric, even when he constantly railed against Israel and promised the "conquest of Qods [Jerusalem]," even when road signs across the country gave not just the distance to the next destination but also to Jerusalem, he had no compunction about signing a secret deal with Israel and the United States to get much-needed ammunition for the war with Iraq. Moreover, then and now American and other Western cities and universities remain the ultimate destination for hundreds of thousands of Iranian exiles and students.

This infatuation began early in the twentieth century as the scientific and commercial dominance of the West became more and more pronounced. A few intellectuals developed a kind of exaggerated, uncritical infatuation with the West. At the same time, as the ideas of radicals like Frantz Fanon and Aime Cesaire came into vogue, anti-Americanism and a critique of Iran's Western orientation also began to develop. Theories about American imperialism and about the United States as the leader of the evil capitalist world were a central component of Soviet cold war propaganda. Memories of August 1953 reinforced these anti-American sentiments. In the decade before the Islamic Revolution, intellectuals like Jalal Al-Ahmad and Ali Shariati advocated a return to "the authentic Iranian self." Al-Ahmad berated Iranian culture and intellectuals for self-loathing and for self-deprecating infatuation with the West. A little known philosophy professor by the name of Ahmad Fardid, taking cues from German philosopher Martin Heidegger, developed a virulent anti-Western, anti-Semitic discourse that had a profound and unfortunate influence on Iranian intellectuals and religious zealots like Ahmadinejad. This intellectual development in Iran paralleled in strikingly similar lines the "Arab predicament" after the shocking defeat of the Six Days' War. Like their Arab counterparts, Fardid, Al-Ahmad, and Shariati all advocated a new identity: more Islamic, more Eastern, less Western. In no small measure, this call to move away from the facile infatuation with the West prepared the ideological ground for the Islamic Revolution of 1979.

But even in the era when the United States was the clear ally of the regime, the Shah sometimes publicly, and more often privately, showed his disdain for the "American way of life" and resentment at the American pressure for democratization. Moreover, he could not forgo the temptation to use Asia, most notably China and Russia, as a foil against the West and the United States. In 1951, Mossadeq nationalized Iranian oil and Great Britain responded by enforcing a full economic embargo against Iran. Desperate for foreign currency and for a new market for Iranian oil, Mossadeq reached out to Communist China in early 1953 and offered to sell it oil at 50 percent of market price. China accepted the offer on the condition that Iran would find a way to deliver the oil to Chinese soil. The plan failed; Iran had no way to deliver the oil. More important, less than three months after the offer, Mossadeq was ousted with the help of the United States.

Six years later the Shah decided to have an Eastern Look of his own. Frustrated with the Eisenhower administration's pressure to democratize and to allot a smaller share of the government budget to military expenditures, Iran secretly invited a high-level Soviet delegation for the purpose of signing a twenty-five-year "friendship and cooperation" treaty. The United States saw the delegation's arrival in Tehran as a form of blackmail, a tactic the Shah had used in the past, although never so audaciously. The Eisenhower administration decided to hold the line against the Shah and his blackmail tactics.

Allan Dulles, director of the CIA, approvingly informed the National Security Council that two of the four Iranian tribal leaders—the Gashgai brothers, living in the United States at the time—had "informed [the United States] that they are proposing to go back to Iran . . . to weaken the Shah."

To make sure the Shah did not miss the message, Eisenhower also sent him a secret letter that was surprisingly "frank and candid" in its tone and its threats. Eisenhower found it "disturbing" that the Shah, instead of "taking a firm position and doing things right" was engaging in "blackmail." He wrote, "I have received information to the effect that your Government is considering the conclusion of a new treaty with the Soviet Union." He added that "in view of the possible far-reaching implications of the matter I should let you know of my concern." Eisenhower emphasized that in his view the Soviet Union, in spite of appearances to the contrary, was still harboring hopes of overthrowing the monarchy in Iran, "separat[ing] Iran from its friends and allies." Regardless of "the actual terms of any new treaty with the Soviet Union, the impact on your friends would be unhappy." The president ended with a clear threat: "I am confident that you would not knowingly take a step which would imperil your country's security and possibly weaken Iran's relations with its proven friends." The Shah walked away from the deal and the Soviets responded by unleashing an unprecedented propaganda campaign against him as a "lackey of American imperialism."

Though the "friendship" treaty was not signed, Iran's attempt to use Russia or even China against the United States continued. In 1965, Iran signed a multi-billion-dollar deal with the Soviet Union for the construction of a steel mill by Soviets in the city of Isfahan in return for Iranian gas exports to Russia. Moreover, Iran began to purchase some military hardware from the Soviets. American attempts to dissuade the Shah from going ahead with the deal came to naught. By the early seventies, much to the consternation of the United States, there were several hundred Soviet advisors and technicians working in Iran.

But the Shah's new geo-strategic game was not limited to improving relations with the USSR. China, too, was a chip the Shah was now willing to play. In the early seventies, Iran and Communist China both had incentives to establish new ties with each other. China abandoned the revolutionary rhetoric of its Cultural Revolution and adopted what it called its new "Three Worlds Theory." The new theory divided the countries around the globe into three worlds: the world of the two superpowers (the Soviet Union and the United States); the world of "medium powers" like Western Europe, Japan, and Australia; and, finally, all other countries, including China and Iran, lumped together in the ubiquitous Third World.

According to this new theory, China supported any country that stood up to either of the two superpowers. Iran, in the new Chinese calculus, was a bulwark against Soviet incursions in the Persian Gulf and thus deserved China's support. China not only ended its financial aid to Iranian Maoist groups, but soon members of the Iranian royal family were being given royal treatment in Beijing. The Shah ordered the government to study the feasibility of selling oil to China. One anomalous consequence of this Iran-China flirtation was that China's leader, Huo Kuo-Feng, turned out to be the last foreign head of state to visit Iran—long after every other government had given up the Shah as politically dead, even "radioactive."

The Chinese government paid for this miscalculation in

the first two years of the revolution, when relations between the Islamic Republic of Iran and China remained frosty. But as relations between the United States and Iran grew increasingly tense and distant, as the two nations began to fight each other through proxies, and as the Soviet Union's occupation of Afghanistan earned Khomeini's disfavor, China found a golden opportunity to fill the vacuum and find a foothold in Iran. But its stubborn support for the Shah in the past became an obstacle to its early expanded influence in Iran.

Two other events allowed Communist China to show its "friendship" with its new Islamic comrades. During the eight-year war between Iran and Iraq, up to 70 percent of Iran's arms came from China. In 1983 China sold $1.3 billion worth of arms to Iran. By 1986, the figure had jumped to $3.1 billion, including Silkworm anti-ship missiles. Moreover, China agreed to sell Iran military technologies and helped set up factories to further Iran's ability to produce its own arms.

Over the last two decades, Iran's trade with China has increased exponentially. In 2007, for example, China's total trade with Iran came to $20.8 billion, while the figure for just the first six months of 2008 reached $14 billion. It is estimated that today at least one hundred Chinese companies work in Iran. For the Islamic regime, reliance on Chinese companies has become a necessity resulting from the U.N. and U.S. sanctions—the same sanctions that earlier the regime had easily circumvented, when the price of oil was over a hundred dollars per barrel. But today, with the price of oil fallen below seventy dollars, it has become impossible for the regime to ignore the increasingly dire consequences of the sanctions. The radicals have tried to turn this necessity into the virtue of the Eastern Look. Virtue or necessity, the Chinese companies are now involved in everything from building an embarrassingly delayed road connecting Tehran to the Caspian Sea to developing oil, gas, manufacturing, mining, and military industries. The fact that China is building a large new embassy in Tehran underscores its vision of a future relationship with Iran.

The most important opportunity for increased "friend-ship" was afforded China when Iran decided to re-launch its nuclear program. Angry with the international community for its silence in the face of Saddam Hussein's use of chemical weapons against Iranian soldiers and helpless Iraqi and Iranian citizens, the regime in Tehran decided to resume the same nuclear program begun by the Shah and shelved by Ayatollah Khomeini as "unnecessary junk." No sooner had Iran com-menced the nuclear program than Rafsanjani made a secret trip to China where he signed deals that overnight made China a key partner in Iran's nuclear technology. Another key actor in the Eastern Look paradigm, Russia, began planning to resume work on the abandoned Bushehr reactor. Germany was contractually obligated to finish that reactor but walked away under pressure from the United States, allowing Russia to move in. Since then, Russia too has increased its stake in every facet of the Iranian economy. Russia anticipates the value of its total trade with Iran to reach $10 billion per year. If the Bushehr reactor is the key symbol of Russia's involve-ment in Iran, the Isfahan Nuclear Research Center, built by China and today considered one of the key components of the regime's nuclear program, is the most important result of the Rafsanjani secret trip that re-launched Iran's nuclear program.

In its attempt to actualize the Eastern Look, Iran has taken a further series of concrete steps. It has already joined the Shanghai Cooperation Organization as an observer; only

China's resistance (at America's behest) has so far blocked Iran's full membership. Furthermore, Iran has suggested a kind of Asia Council that would bring together all major Asian countries, particularly China, Russia, and Iran, and would be defined by its opposition to U.S. hegemony in the continent.

In the last two decades, the Islamic Republic has actively expanded its relations with North Korea, as important for the realization of the Eastern Look as for the success of the regime's nuclear program. North Korea has become for Iran an indispensable and often covert source of assistance for uranium enrichment and missile technologies. In fact, the missile used recently by Iran to put a small satellite in space, with great fanfare and with its traditional self-adulating bombast, was a re-engineered version of a North Korean missile given to Iran a decade earlier. When ties with Communist Asian powers were consolidated, officials in Tehran talked for the first time of forming an Islamabad, New Delhi, Beijing, and Tehran Axis.

The key component of the new Eastern Look—at once its symbol and its indispensible tool—is a pipeline that would eventually connect Iran to China. The first phase of the pipeline, called the Peace Pipeline, would go through Pakistan and India. Iran has been actively trying to convince both countries of the economic wisdom of this project. It has argued that the pipeline, particularly after it has been extended to China, will even help ease tensions between the countries involved. To sweeten the deal, Iran also offered to sell oil and gas to India for twenty-five years at discount prices. Officials of the Iranian regime have estimated that the discounts stipulated in the agreement will cost Iran $210 billion.

But the Peace Pipeline might well be a pipe dream for a

variety of reasons. Not only is it economic folly to limit Iran's market for global commodities like oil and gas to only a portion of that market, but strategic and political tensions and rivalries between China and India, and between Pakistan and India, make the construction of the pipeline unlikely. The continued allure of the Eastern Look for its advocates, despite these obvious tactical obstacles, shows either their dangerous naiveté or the blinding strength of their anti-Americanism.

Ahmadinejad has tried to exaggerate the importance of the Eastern Look policy by fabricating a panicked response by the United States. According to him, the West, in particular the United States, has been so concerned about Iran's plans for the Eastern Look that the CIA masterminded the November 2008 terrorist attacks in Mumbai, India. When the allegation was repeated in two *Keyhan* editorials—a source generally considered to speak informally for Khamenei—it became shockingly clear that the outlandish theory is not just an offshoot of Ahmadinejad's strange conspiratorial (and messianic) vision. The Mumbai attacks, according to this scenario, were meant to abort the possibility of unity between India and Pakistan. While such conspiracy theories are a normal part of Ahmadinejad's paranoid worldview, it is a fact that the United States has been making some efforts to abort the Eastern Look, or at least disrupt plans for construction of the pipeline.

The United States has successfully pressured both China and Russia to walk away from several agreements with Iran, all related to its nuclear program. In addition, Israel—which feels threatened by Iran's nuclear program and which is an increasingly important partner in China's vast investments in the Middle East and elsewhere—has given China one more reason to cautiously ponder its role in Iran's nuclear program.

Even the Bush administration's much maligned nuclear deal with India was partly intended to dissuade India from aligning itself too closely with Iran and with the design for the pipeline.

The much-reported CIA help for the terrorist group called *Jondollah* is also seen by Iran as related to the American effort to destabilize the Iranian regime, making the construction of the pipeline less likely, and thus the realization of the Eastern Look more unlikely. The group is based in the Baluchestan province of Pakistan. At will it crosses the border into the Iranian province of Baluchestan and engages in terrorist acts against the Islamic regime. In October 2009 a suicide bomber belonging to the group killed forty Iranians, including a deputy commander of IRGC. A secure Baluchestan, on both sides of the Iran-Pakistan border, is indispensable for the success of the Peace Pipeline.

But the biggest obstacle to Iran's plans for its Eastern Look has been China's—and to a lesser extent, Russia's—resistance to fully playing the assigned roles. China's far-reaching economic ties to Europe, the United States, and Israel have tempered its temptation to radically increase its stake in Iran. The political constraints of defending an erratic pariah regime whose president calls for an end to the existence of Israel have created some moral and diplomatic constraints to the overwhelming economic incentive for China and Russia to succumb to the Eastern Look temptation. The clear instability in the Iranian regime since the June 12 election might also give China and Russia more reasons to ponder the wisdom of identification with an increasingly authoritarian and brutal regime. Reports that in late December 2009 China delivered, sooner than planned, a large number of armored vehicles intended for use in suppressing demonstrations—ve-

hicles equipped to push back crowds with hot or dyed wa-
ter—have been met with great hostility by members of the
Iranian opposition. Some have threatened China with punishment once the regime has finally fallen.

The willingness of Russia to accept its assigned role is also
less than clear. Putin would enjoy entangling and embarrassing the United States further in its dealings with Iran, but it
is also true that Russia has mounting mutual strategic de-
pendencies with the United States and Israel. Adding a new
layer of complexity is the unresolved question of the division
of the vast oil and gas reserves of the Caspian Sea region.
Iran's desire to keep Russia happy and supportive of the regime's nuclear program has clearly impaired Iran's ability to
demand its rightful share of this vast wealth.

An event that might trigger a change of Chinese or Russian attitudes about the Eastern Look would be preemptive
attacks on Iran's nuclear sites. Experts have indicated that if
such attacks are to be effective, the inexorable "collateral damage" would be the death of thousands of innocent Iranian
civilians. Such action could well afford China or Russia an
occasion to radically expand its stake in Iran. This would go
a long way toward paving the way for the realization of the
Eastern Look. The geo-strategic consequences of this state of
affairs would be as great, and as alarming, as an Iranian regime
armed with a nuclear bomb.

For too long, American policy in Iran has been mired in
a reactive mode. Moreover, for almost two decades the primary focus of all policy has been the nuclear issue. Even the
idea of regime change was more a tool for solving the nuclear
threat than for creating a democratic polity. Overlooked in
this myopic vision has been the equally important strategic
threat embodied in the Eastern Look. Even more crucially

overlooked in this nuclear-fixated vision has been the struggle of the Iranian people to attain democracy and to join the world as a rational and reasonable member of the global community.

Aside from all these geopolitical obstacles to the Eastern Look, a no less formidable obstacle has been the pro-Western and pro-American sentiments of the Iranian people. The favorable disposition of Iranian youth toward the West and America represents the heart and soul of this resistance to turning Eastward. In everything from sartorial style and musical innovation to films and philosophical schools (even the rising trend toward blogging, itself a sign of the rise of self-assertiveness, a requisite component of modernity), the Western and American are immeasurably preferred over the Eastern. The popular music of Mohsen Namjoo—who blends the lyricism of a Leonard Cohen and the musical iconoclasm of Bob Dylan into an innovative reinterpretation of classical Persian music—no less than the ideas of influential young journalists, intellectuals, and activists all exhibit a close reading of Western sources and a fervent desire to adopt, creatively and critically, Western ideas and ideals to the Iranian context. These desires and preferences are America's Trojan horse, helping the Iranian nation realize its century-old dream of democracy. Baskerville's ghost may yet be finally rewarded with the democracy he died for.

If the Obama administration and other Western powers might have reasonably doubted the power and perseverance of the democratic movement in Iran, events since June 12 should have dissipated all doubt. Any American policy that affords any legitimacy to the current beleaguered and brutal ruling triumvirate—the IRGC, Khamenei, and Ahmadinejad—will not only damage democratic prospects in Iran and damage America's standing, it will significantly hinder the resolution of the nuclear impasse. The more threatened the triumvirate feels, the more desperately it needs the nuclear program, if not the nuclear bomb, to survive. The United States must realize that the only resolution to the nuclear problem lies in a transparent and reliable democratic government in Iran. Today that possibility exists more than ever. U.S. relations with Iran will blossom under such a democratic government. With Russia's increasingly aggressive policies in the Caspian region, and with China's overt ambitions for hegemony in the Persian Gulf, the Eastern Look is a dangerous chimera, appealing only to the despots who want to cling to power at any price. On the other hand, an America that is willing to establish equitable relations with a democratic Iran will become a natural ally of an Iran free from clerical despotism and the anti-Americanism that catapulted the clergy into power and kept them there for three decades. And if the history of the twentieth century is any measure, Iran, Egypt, and Turkey are the bellwether states of the Muslim world. A democratic Iran will pollinate other Muslim societies and the winds of that change will transform the face of the Middle East, just as the rise of clerical despotism changed it thirty years ago.

In the months after the rise of the Green Movement, some apologists for the clerical regime maintained that it is but an ephemeral phenomenon. They claimed that the regime, particularly Khamenei himself, is in full control and will weather the storm. Iran today, in their view, is not the Eastern Europe of the early nineties, pregnant with democratic change, but more akin to the China of the early seventies. The apologists argue in favor of a Nixonian policy of open trade with Iran, with no pressure on the regime regarding human rights. What these regime supporters fail to realize is the staying power of the democratic movement and the continued deepening of the fissures within the clerical establishment.

The urgency of the democratic movement and the splits within the regime are in fact rooted in structural defects that lie at the heart of the regime: its economic corruption and incompetence, its ideological sclerosis and anachronism, and its unwillingness to accept the fact that people want democracy and that only democracy can solve Iran's dire social, economic, and political problems.

Khamenei and his allies have tried to use every tool of despotism at their disposal, and none has yet worked. Democracy is the inexorable future of Iran.

The brutality the regime has shown in the past six months has even diminished its standing among its Islamist allies. Some leaders of the Muslim Brotherhood—easily the most powerful Arab Sunni radical group—have begun to gingerly distance themselves from the Iranian regime. Even Shiites of Iraq are increasingly keen on establishing an Iraqi identity, distinct and different from Iran and its Shiite rulers. The menacing "Shiite Crescent" stretching from Iran to the Mediterranean, once forecast, has already begun its decline.

Countries like China and Russia, whose continued support of clerical despotism in Iran has been key to its survival, must realize that siding with despots today—profitable though it might be in the short run—will cost them dearly when the inevitable democratic future arrives. For China and Russia, no less than for the United States and Europe, prudent Iran policy can only be based on a sober analysis of the descending and ascending forces in society. And democracy is truly the ascending idea in Iran.

The Standard Bearer

*Moussavi and the
Green Revolution*

Traditional Iranian husbands, the sort found in the highest ranks of the Islamic Republic, sometimes refer to their wives as "the house." For them, this is not just an expression of their understanding of gender relations. It is viewed as a necessary euphemism, vital protection for a woman's honor. The mere uttering of her name, after all, might compromise her chastity.

It is telling, therefore, that Mir Hossein Moussavi courted and eventually married Zahra Rahnavard. When they met in 1969, Rahnavard was already an acclaimed pioneer in the field of Islamic feminism, as well as a sculptor, critic, and all-around star of the intellectual scene that throbbed in Tehran at that time. But it was her political theories that vaulted her farthest: Rahnavard proffered the kind of critique of patriarchy percolating in the Western academy at the time. Yet she didn't join her sisters in the West in launching an all-out assault on tradition. Yes, Islam has misogynistic elements, she argued in her speeches. But those misogynistic elements are

This chapter was previously published as "The Mousavi Mission" in *The New Republic*, March 11, 2010. Reprinted by permission of *The New Republic*, © 2010, TNR II, LLC.

not necessarily native to Islam. They only prevail because of the male domination of the faith.

For Moussavi, the choice of Rahnavard as his bride was particularly daring—and reveals much about him. Men of his generation, particularly those with a religious proclivity, rarely married assertive intellectuals, let alone intellectuals with greater stature and more impressive curricula vitae. Throughout his career, friends and foes have referred to him as "the husband of Zahra Rahnavard."

Zahra Rahnavard's husband, of course, has emerged as a towering figure of the Iranian democratic movement, the man whose campaign inspired so much hope and whose thwarted election has unleashed an unprecedented wave of protest. Yet, for all his centrality to these events, he remains essentially a fuzzy figure in most press accounts.

At first glance, Moussavi's long career is a riddle: How could he possibly represent the forces for liberalism and democracy when he served as such a loyal foot soldier in Ayatollah Khomeini's revolution? During his eight years as prime minister, back in the 1980s, the regime committed terrible atrocities. It was involved in a brutal military conflict: an eight-year war that Iran prolonged needlessly.

But, even without this history, Moussavi would be enigmatic. His aversion to the limelight, soft voice, and natural shyness make him a perfect tabula rasa. At times amid the tumult, Moussavi seemed nothing more than a passive actor in all the grand historic drama of the Green Revolution. Did he ever intend to unleash a movement challenging the very core of the Islamic Republic? Or was he simply carried along by the enthusiasms of his supporters?

There are enough clues lurking in the annals that a profile of the man begins to emerge. There are simple facts like his courtship of Zahra Rahnavard—a defiant act that prefigured a lifetime of subtly bucking the forces of reaction. The Green Movement's showdown with the regime was, in fact, the culmination of Moussavi's long struggle.

Mir Hossein Moussavi Khamenei was born in 1941 in the northwestern city of Khameneh. He is, as his full surname suggests, a distant relative of Supreme Leader Ali Khamenei, his nemesis. His father was a tea merchant of modest means. When he left home for the newly established National University in Tehran, he didn't land in the coveted schools of medicine, engineering, or law. Still, it was pretty impressive for a kid from the provinces to win entry into the Faculty of Art and Architecture. At the time Moussavi started, the National University was filled with children of the upper class. But, before he finished there, the state nationalized the institution and diversified its socioeconomic composition. It became a hotbed of opposition to the Shah. Moussavi, in fact, helped create and shape the school's Islamic student association, one such anti-regime outpost.

By the time he received a master's degree in architecture in the late sixties, the politics of the Iranian intelligentsia had begun to shift. Modern men and women no longer equated Islam with superstition. Moussavi began hanging out at the Hosseiniye Ershad, a meeting place built by some of the more moderate supporters of the Ayatollah Khomeini. The whole program at Hosseiniye Ershad was intended to appeal to the modern sensibilities of the urban, educated middle classes who might otherwise have avoided mosques—people very much like Moussavi and Rahnavard.

One of Hosseiniye Ershad's main draws was a fiery orator called Ali Shariati. Hardly a man of great erudition, Shariati had a gift for ideological alchemy, which perhaps explains his outsize influence. While studying in Paris, he had inhaled all the revolutionary doctrines of the era. His lectures in Tehran attempted to synthesize Marx and Mohammad, Imam Hussein (the quintessence of the Shiite cult of martyrdom), and Che Guevara. It all added up to a sort of liberation theology. His eclectic brand of Shiism promised to usher in revolution in this world and salvation in the next.

Shariati's inherently incongruent ideology was emblematic of the incongruent political coalition that came together in Iran's pre-revolutionary days. Khomeini himself sometimes usurped Marxist rhetoric in his fusillades against the United States and capitalism, as well as in his encomiums for the poor. In his critique of the traditional Shiite clergy—a group that he described as sclerotic and superstitious, enemies of progress and true Islam—Shariati had exempted Khomeini, praising him for his fierce fight against despotism and colonialism.

This was a message that resonated with Moussavi. Like Shariati, he boiled over with anger at the *ancien régime*. He too attacked the Shah's despotism and dependence on the West. (He wrote essays under the nom de guerre Rahro, the seeker, or traveler.) Like his mentor Shariati, Moussavi grew enamored of Khomeini, especially in the euphoric glow of revolution. But, ever since his days at Hosseiniye Ershad, we can also see in Moussavi traces of Shariati's fulminations against conservative, traditional mullahs, a dislike that long predates the Green Movement.

In some respects, Shariati (who died about two years before the Shah's regime toppled) was one of the most important ideologues of the revolution. In his inconsistent but seductive rhetoric were hints of the futile promise of the revolution—the idea that a new regime might manage to fulfill the greatest hopes of the left-wing radicals, the Qom-based clerics, and the middle classes who hoped to synthesize those poles. Only in the face of the Shah's repression could the tensions inherent in this coalition be sublimated. And, even then, they were real. Before Shariati's death, Khomeini denounced him and effectively banned him from speaking at the Ershad.

These ideological tensions remain the dominant fault line in Iranian politics. The reform movements—embodied first by President Mohammad Khatami and later represented in the leadership of the Green Movement—are, in essence, the wing of the revolution's unwieldy coalition that felt betrayed by the despotic rightward turn of the regime.

By any measure, the rise of a little-known architect and newspaper editor to the highest ranks of the new regime was surprising, even meteoric. But, by the time of the revolution, Moussavi had built a reputation as a leading intellectual and man of unquestionable pieties. And at that moment the regime needed a façade that projected a spirit of inclusion that could ballast its far-flung coalition. With both his demeanor and his ideological roots in the Ershad, Moussavi exuded exactly those reassuring qualities. What's more, he had a powerful friend and patron in Ayatollah Mohammad Beheshti, the secretary of the Islamic Revolution Council. Shortly after the revolution, Beheshti, with an assist from Ali Akbar Hashemi Rafsanjani and Ali Khamenei, organized the Islamic Republican Party and named Moussavi editor-in-chief of the party's newspaper. When Beheshti and more than seventy other top leaders of the regime were killed by terrorist attacks, Moussavi, having only served a brief tenure as foreign minister, began his rapid ascent to the premiership.

The great struggle in Iranian politics that broke out in

the summer of 2009 pit Moussavi against Ali Khamenei. It
has been that way, more or less, from the birth of the regime.
During much of Moussavi's tenure as prime minister, Khamenei was president. In those days, authority rested primarily
in the hands of the prime minister, while the presidency was
a largely symbolic office. Khamenei, however, never accepted
such limits. He consistently trespassed onto Moussavi's turf,
attempting to grab power and interfere. Genuine ideological
differences undergirded this rivalry. Khamenei was increasingly aligned with the conservative clergy and with the forces
in the bazaar who were opposed to the state's domination of
the economy and demanded a freer hand in making profits
from their activities. His ideological guru was a man named
Navvab Safavi, the founder of the Islamic terrorist group Fa-
dayan Islam (Martyrs of Islam). Moussavi, on the other hand,
pushed for the state to take a more activist role in managing
the economy.

As president, more than once, Khamenei tried to oust
Moussavi. He solicited the help of other top clerics like Rafsanjani and Ayatollah Hossein Ali Montazeri. Both declined
to join the effort. When Khamenei won reelection in 1985,
he wrote Khomeini a letter detailing his voluminous complaints against Moussavi. Though the letter has never been
made public, we can deduce from published reports that the
complaints were both personal and ideological: he railed
against Moussavi's technocratic inclinations and his toleration
of artists and intellectuals who were not, in the strict sense,
Islamist. But Khamenei's many attempts to rid himself of
Moussavi came to naught. Khomeini defended Moussavi. In
an implicit attack on Khamenei and other critics, Khomeini
once declared that Moussavi's critics could not even run a
bakery—in other words, what impressed Khomeini most

about Moussavi was his management of the economy. But Khomeini was not Moussavi's only champion. The Revolutionary Guard (IRGC) also adored him. His reputation rested on his probity. He organized a system of food rationing that was generally free of corruption. And there was a broad sense that Moussavi resisted the pocket-lining temptation that befell so many of his comrades.

Two clouds, however, hovered over his years in office. The first was his role in the Iran-Contra affair. Although he didn't greet Oliver North when the Marine arrived in Tehran, allegedly bearing a cake and a Bible, Moussavi was in the thick of negotiations with him. According to some accounts, he was one of three top Iranian officials—the others were Rafsanjani and Khamenei—who brokered the deal to trade the release of American hostages in Lebanon in return for the sale of much-needed U.S. arms. Working so closely with the Great Satan took its toll on Moussavi's reputation. (While Rafsanjani also paid a price for his role in the affair, Khamenei successfully kept his own role secret.)

By far, the most severe (and most repeated) criticism about Moussavi involves his possible role in the 1988 execution of close to 4,000 members of the Mojahedeen-e Khalg-e Iran (MEK), a political party that had split with Khomeini and violently opposed him. Most of the slaughtered were simply political prisoners. What role did Moussavi play in this episode? At best, he was ignorant of the event, which is what he recounts. We also have an account of the episode in the memoirs of the recently deceased Ayatollah Montazeri. When Montazeri strenuously objected to the massacre, Khomeini removed him as his designated successor. Montazeri's memoir makes clear that many in the top tier of government—including then-President Ali Khamenei—were unaware of the murders. Moreover, Montazeri's fervent support for Moussavi's presidential campaign enhances the credibility of his claim of ignorance. Still, even if he can be absolved of this crime, he couldn't have survived so long in one of the top positions of this regime without making many other sacrifices of his conscience.

With the death of Ayatollah Khomeini in 1989, Moussavi's political career came to an abrupt end. Ali Khamenei became the country's supreme leader and, in the constitutional revision that made his ascension possible, he backed a successful campaign to eliminate the role of the prime minister entirely. Exiled from power by the politicians, Moussavi retreated into aesthetics—painting, architecture, serving as president of the national Academy of the Arts.

It is always difficult, even dangerous, to extract ideological insights from an artist's *oeuvre*. But in Iran art rarely exists within a vacuum. Traditional Islam forbids the reproduction of a human face. Such creation, it believes, must remain the monopoly of Allah. As a result, Islamic art has largely sublimated the aesthetic impulse into formalism—ornate calligraphy, arabesque tiles, and, of course, Persian rugs. Moussavi's paintings are well within this tradition. They make no effort to represent reality. They consist of simple lines, beguilingly arranged—sometimes in the style of Piet Mondrian, only more muted, and other times resembling the simple, graceful curves of, say, a Persian dome.

His paintings and architecture can be read as a reflection of the man's own soft-spoken tendencies. But what's important is their eclecticism, their openness to an array of influences. In architecture, he is an avid fan of Renzo Piano, the modernist architect who co-designed the famed Pompidou Center in Paris. What Piano did with buildings—expose the structural armature of a building instead of hiding it behind aesthetic façades—is the sort of transparency that appeals to Moussavi's democratic instincts. In the many buildings he has designed, Moussavi has been as much inspired by elements of the Piano style as the traditional Iranian style. His paintings and buildings, no less than his politics, all point to a man not only well-informed about Western aesthetic modernism and political modernity but willing and able to combine them with native elements.

During his long hiatus from electoral politics, Moussavi deepened the ties he had established with Iran's intellectual elite—from Islamist reformers to secular artists—and these ties intensified his liberal instincts. In 1997, when the emerging reformist camp first tried to mount a presidential campaign, it attempted to draft Moussavi. He did not accept. Some suggest he did not believe Khamenei would allow his candidacy to pass the vetting process in the Guardian Council (a body of twelve men that must approve every candidate that appears on any ballot). Others say that he was blackmailed by conservatives who threatened to publish youthful images of his wife without the Islamic hijab. While he did not become a candidate, he and his wife were close advisers to the ultimate reform candidate and winner, Mohammad Khatami.

The Khatami period was at once an era of great openness and great disappointment. And the fact that the theocracy undermined the country's duly elected president—arresting many of his aides, shuttering sympathetic newspapers, and rejecting as inimical to Islamic *sharia* nearly every law passed by his supporters in the parliament—highlighted the fundamental hopelessness of working within the system, or, at least, the necessity of radically reforming it. After Khatami left office in 2005 and then watched the Ahmadinejad presidency in horror, he contemplated running for his old job last year. But a Khatami candidacy was a risk that Khamenei was not willing to take. And, as the regime pressured Khatami to pull out of the race, Moussavi stepped in to fill the reformist void. It seems that Khamenei viewed him as an acceptably harmless risk to his rule. With Moussavi's low-key demeanor and long absence from politics, it was hard to imagine him posing much of a threat to Ahmadinejad.

But then something happened on the way to the polls. With the unprecedented participation of his wife—a novelty in the Islamic regime—and with a simple motto of "every citizen a campaign headquarter," Moussavi unleashed an enthusiastic, Internet-savvy campaign that paralyzed the regime. His performance in televised debates helped win over the uncommitted middle. In one debate, Ahmadinejad wielded a sheet of paper, implying that it contained something incriminating about Zahra Rahnavard, and asked menacingly more than once, "Do you want me to show it?" Eventually, Ahmadinejad did question Rahnavard's academic credentials. Rahnavard responded vehemently to the slanders, proudly defending her scholarly record. Moussavi rallied the support of popular celebrities (from the filmmaker Dariush Mehrjui to soccer players). He harvested the accumulating resentment against the regime's economic incompetence and cultural hooliganism. In one of his campaign films made by a top secular director, Moussavi declares that, if elected, he would end the days of governance by "soothsayers and palm readers," replacing ignorance and arrogance with experts and reason. This message won the support of not just youth and the women's movement, but also the anemic private sector, which helped underwrite the campaign.

Even more remarkable than his campaign was his stewardship of the Green Movement that protested the stolen election. The movement is composed of supporters of nearly every political persuasion, from reformists who just want to restore the regime to its "golden age" to those who want to start anew. Moussavi has had to temper the radicalism of the latter and surmount the conservatism of the former. At the same time, he has been careful not to say anything that could be construed as sedition and land him in jail. Moussavi managed to maintain his coalition through the use of a broad, simple message. Millions marched around the slogan: "What happened to my vote?" Through it all, Moussavi displayed astonishing calm. He issued seventeen statements and gave a number of interviews. Reading them as a collection, one can see the arc of his thinking—increasing alienation from the regime and growing dedication to democratic values. In an interview in late February 2010, published on his Web site, *Kalame*, he defiantly, albeit obliquely, compared Khamenei's despotism with that of the Shah. Today's despotism, he declared, is a continuation of royalist despotism. It was a perfect summation of the disappointment felt so deeply by so many of the original revolutionaries.

The regime did its best to make life miserable for Moussavi and his wife. It arrested his brain trust and forced some to "confess" to egregious crimes. When leaving their home, the couple were more than once assaulted by regime goons. In the press, they were the subject of a steady campaign of slander that, among other attacks, implied that Moussavi wasn't even a Muslim. Sites officially tied to the Revolutionary Guard accused Moussavi's wife of "holding in secret the same creed" as Shirin Ebadi, Iran's Nobel laureate. "She is a Zionist Bahai, and has problems with Islam."

Yet, in all of this, the regime refrained from arresting

Moussavi. In an otherwise brutal crackdown, this restraint was an obvious bow to pragmatism. The regime resisted possibly turning Moussavi into the Nelson Mandela of the movement: a prisoner who would symbolize the regime's horrors, a cause célèbre for world opinion. With his soft voice and modesty, his commitment to nonviolence and reason, he was the one martyr that the regime could not afford.

Notes

Chapter One. The Iranian Purgatory

1. A couple of weeks after the electoral heist, *Etemad Melli* was closed on a technicality and has still not been allowed to resume publication.

Chapter Two. The Myth of the Great Satan

1. PRO (Public Record Office), "Iranian International Situation, 12 October 1978," PREM 16/1719.

2. CIA, "Mohammad Reza Pahlavi, Shah of Iran, 23 October 1978." I obtained a copy though a Freedom of Information Act request.

3. Marvin Zonis, *Majestic Failure: The Fall of the Shah* (Chicago: University of Chicago Press, 1991). Zonis used psychological theories to argue that the men and women the Shah relied on for his "selfhood" were all gone by the time of the revolution.

4. CIA, "Profile of the Shah," Freedom of Information Act request.

5. Gen. Huyser was a NATO commander. Like nearly every high-ranking U.S. official dealing with Iran in those days, he published a memoir, *Mission to Tehran* (New York: Harper Collins, 1987).

6. NSA (National Security Archives), No. 603, Bureau of Intelligence and Research, Department of State, "Studies in Political Dynamics in Iran," Secret Intelligence Report 13.

7. William Shawcross, *The Shah's Last Ride* (London: Pan Books, 1989), 99.

8. PRO, "30 October 1978, Prime Minister's Office to Foreign Ministry," PREM 16/1719.

9. Bani-Sadr now lives in exile, protected by the French government against the Islamic regime's potential assassins; Qotb-Zadeh was sent to the firing squad on the charge of attempting a coup against Khomeini; and Yazdi is a marginalized member of the opposition in Iran today. He was arrested in the aftermath of the post-election protest.

10. NSA, No. 1298, Sullivan, "Understanding the Shiite Islamic Movement," American Embassy, Tehran, Feb. 2, 1979.

Chapter Three. Purposes Mistook

1. Charles Kurzman, *The Unthinkable Revolution in Iran* (Cambridge: Harvard University Press, 2004).

2. Two studies, one by poet Mohammad Mokhtari and one by Mehdi Bazorgan, first prime minister of the Islamic Republic of Iran, came up with slightly different percentages about the content of the slogans. For a discussion of the two studies, see Mohsen Milani, *The Making of the Islamic Revolution*, 2nd rev. ed. (Boulder: Westview Press, 1999), 136.

3. For a brief account of his life, see Rezazedeh Shafag, *Howard Baskerville: The Story of an American Who Died in the Cause of Iranian Freedom and Independence* (Cambridge, Mass.: Ty Aur Press, 2008). The monograph is a translation of an article that had earlier appeared in Persian in *Tehran Times*, December 14, 1959.

4. NSA, no. 244, "Current Foreign Relations," April 11, 1979.

5. Richard Hofstadter, "The Paranoid Style in American Politics," *Harper's*, November 1964, 77–86. The seminal essay was later republished as part of a book, *The Paranoid Style in American Politics and Other Essays* (Cambridge: Harvard University Press, 1996).

6. PRO, "The British Hand," September 25, 1978, PREM/16/179.

7. U.S. embassy in Tehran, "Alternative Views from the Provinces," in *Asnad-e Laneye Jasusi* (Documents from the Den Of Spies), (Tehran, n.d.), vol. 16. This multi-volume collection included reprints of thousands of pages of confidential documents students found when they occupied the U.S. embassy. It has been said that some of the most sensitive documents were earlier sent out and some were shredded as the students were staging their assault. Faced with shredded documents, the Iranian regime is reported to have used the services of carpet weavers to piece together most of them. In their reprints, they look distinctly different than those found intact.

8. George Ball, "Issues and Implications of the Iranian Crisis," December 1978, "George Ball Papers" in Princeton University Library, Seeley G. Mudd Manuscript Library, Box 30, Doc. MC031.

9. Y. Armajani, "Alborz College," *Encyclopaedia Iranica*.

10. For a detailed account of Soviet machinations, based on Soviet archives, see Jamil Hasanli, *At the Dawn of the Cold War: The Soviet-American Crisis Over Iranian Azerbaijan, 1941–1946* (Lanham, Md.: Rowman and Littlefield, 2006).

11. U.S. Department of State, *Foreign Relations of the United States, 1952–1954* (Washington, DC: U.S. Government Printing, 1989), 695.

12. Ibid., 751.

13. Ibid., 754.

14. U.S. Department of State, *Foreign Relations of the United States, 1952–1954* (Washington, DC: U.S. Government Printing, 1989), 695.

15. Ibid., 606.

16. Ibid., 613.

17. NSA, no. 369, "Political Internal Issues."

18. PRO, "Tehran to Foreign Office, 6 July 1978," FCO 8/3184.

19. Ball, "Issues and Implications," 3.

20. JFK Library (John F. Kennedy Presidential Library), FRUS, vol. XVIII, Microfilm Supplements, "Tehran to State Department, May 13, 1961."

21. JFK Library, "Tehran to State Department, May 14, 1961."

22. CIA, "Profile of the Shah, 28 September 1973," Freedom of Information Act request, Ref. F-2006-00113.

23. JFK Library, "Tehran to State Department, May 13, 1961."

24. There are several scholarly reports about the land reform and they are more or less in consensus that Arsanjani had a radicalizing effect. See, for example, Afsaneh Najmabadi, *Land Reform and Social Change in Iran* (Salt Lake City: University of Utah Press, 1987), 83.

25. JFK Library, "Tehran to State, June 28, 1961."

26. Ibid.

27. JFK Library, "25 May 1961 Memo for Philip Talbott."

28. Abolhassan Ebtehaj, *The Memoirs of Abolhassan Ebtehaj* (London: Paka Print, 1991), 853–857.

29. This was the most important result of the Shah's visit to the White House in 1962. For details of their last joint press

conference, see JFK Library, NSC Box 116, "Robert Komer to Bundy, April 23, 1962."

30. NSA, no. 9799, U.S. embassy, Tehran, "End of Tour Report, August 4, 1975."

31. For a detailed account of the role of the U.S. embassy and CIA in these developments, see Abbas Milani, *Persian Sphinx: Amir Abbas Hoveyda and the Riddle of the Iranian Revolution* (Washington, DC: Mage Publishers, 1999), particularly the chapters "Progressive Circle" and "White Revolution," 135–171.

32. NSA, no. 2048, "Religious Leaders Fear Departure of the Shah," January 9, 1969.

33. Ball, "Issues and Implications," 9.

34. Asadollah Alam, *Yadashtha-ye Alam*, [The Diaries of Asadollah Alam], ed. by Alinaghi Alikhani (Washington, DC: Ibex Publishers, 2008), vol. 6, 21–23.

35. NSA, "A Brief Overview of U.S.-Iran Relations," 27. The report was prepared in the early 1980s; it has no author or indication of who commissioned it.

36. Ball, "Issues and Implications."

37. For a more or less impartial description of the group, see Ervand Abrahamian, *The Iranian Mojahedin* (New Haven: Yale University Press, 2009). The Murphy Report prepared for the State Department describing the group as a terrorist organization is a critical account of its work. The group has taken the State Department to federal court four times to have its name removed from the list, all to no avail.

38. For a detailed account of this romance, see Janet Afary and Kevin B. Anderson, *Foucault and the Iranian Revolution: Gender and the Seductions of Islamism* (Chicago: University of Chicago Press, 2005).

39. Mohammad Reza Pahlavi, *Answer to History* (New York: Stein and Day, 1980), 93–97.

40. PRO, "Embassy in Tehran to Foreign Office, 8 September 1978," FCO 8/3184.

41. PRO, "Embassy in Tehran to Foreign Office, November 9, 1978," FCO 8/3184.

About the Author

Abbas Milani was born in Iran and educated in the United States. He taught at Tehran University's Faculty of Law and Political Science until 1986. For many years he was the chair of the Department of History and Political Science at Notre Dame De Namur University. Since 2002 he has been at Stanford University, where he co-directs the Iran Democracy Project at the Hoover Institution; since 2005 he has been the Hamid and Christina Moghadam Director of Iranian Studies at Stanford. He has published more than twenty books, numerous articles, and monographs in both Persian and English. His memoir, *Tales of Two Cities: A Persian Memoir* (Mage Publisher) was a *San Francisco Chronicle* best seller; his translation of his own *Persian Sphinx: Amir Abbas Hoveyda and the Riddle of the Iranian Revolution* went through more than twenty printings before being banned by the Iranian regime in February 2010. His *Eminent Persians: The Men and Women Who Made Modern Iran, 1941–1979* (Syracuse University Press, 2009) offers biographical sketches of 150 of modern Iran's most influential artists, politicians, and entrepreneurs. His work has been translated into many languages. His *Peacock Prince, a Political Life of the Shah* will soon be published by Palgrave Press.

 *Herbert and Jane Dwight Working Group on Islamism and the International Order*

HOOVER INSTITUTION **STANFORD UNIVERSITY**

The Herbert and Jane Dwight Working Group on Islamism and the International Order seeks to engage in the task of reversing Islamic radicalism through reforming and strengthening the legitimate role of the state across the entire Muslim world. Efforts will draw on the intellectual resources of an array of scholars and practitioners from within the United States and abroad, to foster the pursuit of modernity, human flourishing, and the rule of law and reason in Islamic lands—developments that are critical to the very order of the international system.

The Working Group is chaired by Hoover fellows Fouad Ajami and Charles Hill with an active participation of Director John Raisian. Current core membership includes Russell A. Berman, Abbas Milani, and Shelby Steele, with contributions from Zeyno Baran, Reuel Marc Gerecht, Ziad Haider, John Hughes, Nibras Kazimi, Habib Malik, and Joshua Teitelbaum.

Index

Stalin, Josef, 34, 46–47, 57–58
State Department's Bureau of
  Intelligence and Research, 33, 65
Status of Forces Agreement, 76–77
Strait of Hormuz, 79–80, 104
"Students Following the Line of
  Imam," 45
Sullivan, William H., 77
Sunni, 8–9, 13
suppression, 48
surveillance, 14, 48
Survey of Persian Art (Pope), 54

Taleghani, Mahmoud (Ayatollah),
  86
Tehran; conference, 57;
  demonstrations in, 19–20. *See also*
  United States embassy in Tehran
terrorism, x–xi, 85, 91, 93–94, 102,
  113, 114, 123–24. *See also specific
  terrorist groups*
Three Worlds Theory, 109
de Tocqueville, Alexis, 10
totalitarianism, 12
trans-national railroad, 56
Truman, Harry S., 58, 60
Tudeh Party, 40, 58–59, 61, 84–85
Twelfth Imam, 42, 46, 55

umma, 20
U.N. *See* United Nations
United Nations (U.N.), 58, 94–95,
  99–100
United States (U.S.), 35, 51–52, 79,
  91, 108–9; in Azerbaijan crisis,
  role of, 59; clerical regime and,
  91; Constitutional Revolution
  and, 42; Eastern Look, efforts to
  abort, 113–14; as First New
  Nation, 22; hostage crisis,
  investigation of, 50; interest in
  political development in Iran, 50;
  Iran and, people of, 10–11;
  Iranian democratic movement

and, 43–44; Iran's domestic
  politics, role in, 50–54, 65; Iran's
  image of, 55; Islamic Revolution
  of 1979 and, 52; Khamenei's
  distrust/dislike of, roots of, 8–10;
  Khomeini alliance with, 31,
  81–82; Khomeini to power, role
  in preparing grounds for rise of,
  49–50; nuclear program in Iran
  and, 103–4, 117; policy in Iran,
  34, 97, 115
policy proposals, 65–66; Shah and,
  rise and fall of, 26–27, 49; Shah
  in, 95–96; Shah's relations with,
  63–64, 88, 90–91, 107; visa
  status of Confederation of Iranian
  Students and, 88–89
United States embassy in Tehran,
  35, 37, 45, 52, 66, 81;
  "Alternative Views from the
  Provinces," 133n7. *See also*
  hostage crisis
United States-Iran relations, 7, 25,
  59–60, 94, 117; history of recent,
  8–10
mid-19th century, 53–54; onset of
  cold war and, 57–58; post-2009
  elections, 7–8, 18; problems
  plaguing, 91–92; World War II
  and, 55–58
United States-Israeli relations, 30
United States-UN embargo, 94–95
uranium enrichment activities, 15,
  99–100, 104, 112

Velayat-e Fagih, 9–10, 35–36, 44–
  45, 47
velvet revolution, 3, 7, 9, 21, 50
Venezuela, 15
Vietnam War, 79
violence, 11, 47

wars, East-West, of renaissance
  period, 105; "just," 11. *See also
  specific wars*